LOVE

THE GREAT QUEST

Nancy Dufresne

DUFRESNE MINISTRIES
PUBLICATIONS

Love: The Great Quest
ISBN: 978-0-940763-01-2
Copyright © 2020, 2023 by Dufresne Ministries

Published by:
Dufresne Ministries Publications
P.O. Box 1010
Murrieta, CA 92564
www.dufresneministries.org

1-2500   2-3000

Cover design: Grant Dufresne
Cover graphic image: Envato Elements, Graphic Goods
Bio photo: Bree Hokana © Dufresne Ministries

WORLD HARVEST
BIBLE TRAINING CENTER
M U R R I E T A · C A L I F O R N I A

TRAINING BELIEVERS TO MOVE WITH THE WORD & THE SPIRIT

FOR MORE INFO OR TO SUBMIT AN APPLICATION ONLINE, GO TO

WWW.WHBTC.ORG

OR CONTACT OUR OFFICE AT (951) 696-9258, EXT. 202

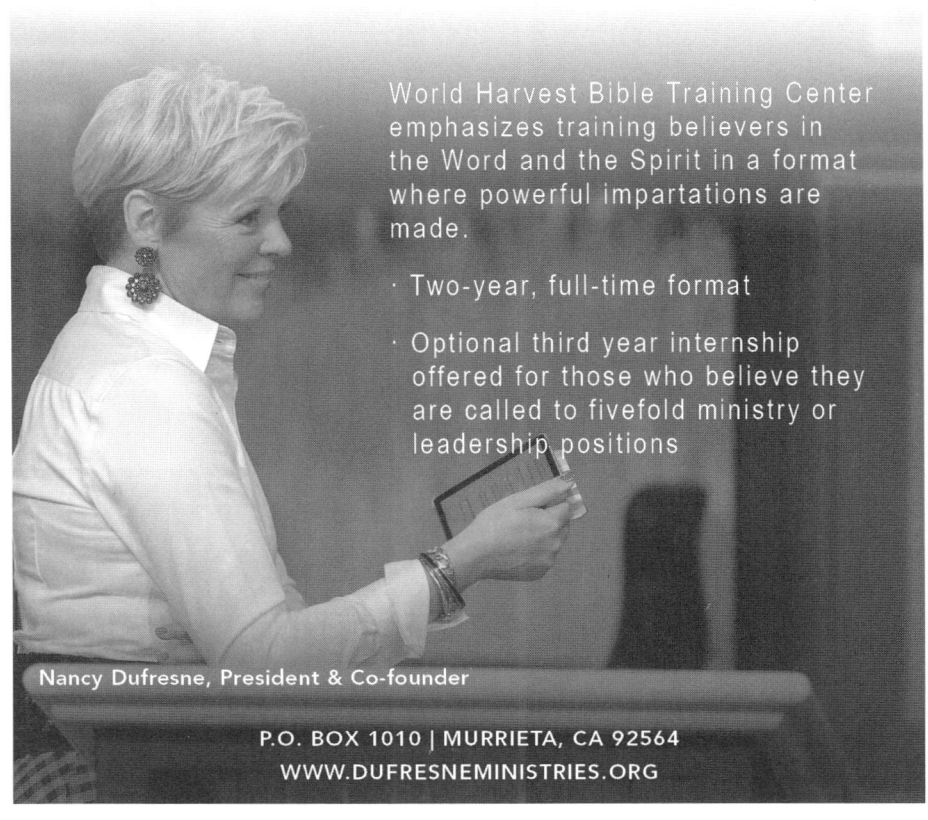

Books by Nancy Dufresne

Daily Healing Bread From God's Table

His Presence Shall Be My Dwelling Place

The Healer Divine

Victory in the Name

*There Came a Sound From Heaven:
The Life Story of Dr. Ed Dufresne*

Visitations From God

Responding to the Holy Spirit

God: The Revealer of Secrets

A Supernatural Prayer Life

Causes

I Have a Supply

*Fit for the Master's Use:
A Handbook for Raising Godly Children*

A Sound, Disciplined Mind

Knowing Your Measure of Faith

The Greatness of God's Power

Peace: Living Free From Worry

Following the Holy Spirit

An Apostle of the Anointing:
A Biography of Dr. Ed Dufresne

Victory Over Grief & Sorrow

Answer It!

The Price of the Double Portion Anointing

Worship

Books in Spanish

Pan Diario de Sanidad de la Mesa de Dios
(Spanish edition of *Daily Healing Bread*)

Contents

SECTION 1 — GOD'S LOVE FOR US

1. Human Love vs. Divine Love 11
2. Know & Believe the Love 19
3. The Love Realm 29
4. Filled With God 33
5. Perfect Love Casts Out Fear 45
6. Correction: A Flow of Love 51

SECTION 2 — OUR LOVE FOR GOD

7. "If a Man Love Me..." 57
8. Love & Obedience 63

SECTION 3 — LOVE IN US

9. Growing in Love 73
10. Love & Faith 79
11. Love & Forgiveness 85
12. Love & Healing 91
13. Love & Prosperity 99

SECTION 4 — OUR LOVE FOR OTHERS

14. Love & the Home 109
15. Love & Ministry 115
16. Love's Way 121
17. Love Defined 131
    Compiled List of Love Definitions 151

Prayer of Salvation 159
How To Be Filled With the Holy Spirit 161
Prayer To Receive the Holy Spirit 165

SECTION 1
GOD'S LOVE FOR US

"Eagerly pursue and seek to acquire [this] LOVE [make it your aim, YOUR GREAT QUEST]...."

– 1 Corinthians 14:1 (AMPC)

Chapter 1

Human Love vs. Divine Love

Love is the cure for the flaws of man. It is the solution to human difficulties. Love is the highest and best way to walk, and it is the way we are commanded to live. *"Be ye therefore followers of God, as dear children; And walk in love..."* (Eph. 5:1 & 2).

Especially in these last days, opposition and circumstances unique to these times will arise, so we must walk in the revelation of love, for it is the way we will overcome and move forward as victors in these perilous days. Jesus has made us victor and master over all opposition, so as we move forward in love, love victories await us!

"Eagerly pursue and seek to acquire [this] love [make it your aim, YOUR GREAT QUEST]..." (1 Cor. 14:1, AMPC).

One translation states, *"Let love be your highest goal."*

"...Follow after...love..." (1 Tim. 6:11).

Romans 5:5 tells us, *"...the love of God is shed abroad in our hearts by the Holy Ghost which is given unto us."* Every believer has the love of God in them; therefore, we are to follow the way of love. Love will lead and govern us, and we are to make it our quest to follow the way love leads; as we do, we will lay hold of all love offers us. As we follow after love, it will define how we see things – showing us God's view. It will lead us down the most thrilling paths, show us the most grand and highest views, fill our lives with all that is best, help us to live the best versions of ourselves, and enable us to be a blessing to many along the way. Love offers us the best life – the God-life.

Men pursue many things in this life. Some pursue fame, wealth, professional success, prestige, power, and influence. But without knowing the Father of love and being a part of His great love family, all men – no matter what accomplishments are achieved in life – will only end up on the dead-end road of disappointment and emptiness.

Love offers man more – it offers him the best life. Yet many are speeding down life's road at such a pace, that they miss, overlook, or are too busy to notice what love is offering them. They are in pursuit of their own dreams and plans. But God made a love plan for every man, and all who hunger for it and will receive it can have all love offers them.

It is our great privilege to do as commanded, *"EAGERLY PURSUE and seek to acquire [this] love [make it your aim, YOUR GREAT QUEST]...."*

His Love Representatives

As we are commanded in John 13:34 & 35, *"A new commandment I give unto you, That ye love one another; AS*

I HAVE LOVED YOU, that ye also love one another. By this shall all men know that ye are my disciples, if ye have love one to another."

The love Jesus introduced to the earth is the same love we now possess and are to bring to others. We are carrying on His great love walk on this earth. Now that He is seated at the right hand of the Father, carrying on His divine work, He is ministering to us, enabling us to take His place on the earth.

When Jesus stated, "I only say what I hear My Father say. I only do what I see My Father do," He was letting us know that His words and actions were directed and empowered from the Throne. Now God is doing that through us; the Throne is to direct our words and actions, for we are now taking Jesus' place in the earth. We are to feel the same love and compassion for people that He feels. We are to be His constant love representatives here on the earth.

Two Loves Compared

In writing on love, there is a definite sense of the largeness of the subject and all that is connected to it. To undertake it is to attempt to write of God Himself. The subject is vast – as vast as God Himself.

The Word tells us that God IS love (1 John 4:8 & 16). Love is not simply a characteristic of God, but it is His essence. *He is nothing as much as He is love.* To articulate that in natural, human words and give it due honor can seem daunting, so with reverence and reliance upon the great Helper, the Holy Spirit, I begin.

To address this divine topic justly, I will write of love and the different directions it flows:

(1) God's love for us
(2) Our love for God
(3) Love in us
(4) Our love for others

To correctly understand love, we must first realize that there are two kinds of love, and they are on polar opposite ends of the spectrum. One fails, the other succeeds.

There is human love that is natural in origin. This is the love that every human being operates in from birth. This is a love based on the natural man, the flesh, on feelings, emotions, temporal things, and temporal settings. It may seem to be a strong starter, but it's a poor finisher. It has limited endurance; it will give up and quit. It will abandon people, obligations, and responsibilities – it's a quitter. It may start with good intentions, but those intentions weaken and fail when pressure shows up. It doesn't have "the stuff" to hold up under pressure – it will lose strength and fail, giving up. This human love will turn to hate; it will turn on someone, strike back in anger, fling words of hurt and hate at others, fight to get its own way, put itself first, and do whatever is necessary to end up on top, for it is a selfish love. This love turns homes and lives into war zones.

This human love is flawed, but it is the only love flow available for the unsaved man to draw on. Human love is the outflow of a man without God. It is the flow of the spiritually dead man – one separated from God – and one whose nature is all wrong. He has a sin nature in him.

The other kind of love is divine love. It is the God-kind of love that found its entrance into the earth with Jesus. He introduced and walked in this new kind of love, making it available to every man who will receive it.

Divine love is not based on man's flesh, feelings, or emotions, for it originates with God – not man. It is the essence of God Himself; it is Him and His flow. Every movement God makes is a love movement. Every word God speaks is a love word. Every thought of God is a love thought. God IS love. There is no separation between God and divine love – they are one and the same. God IS love, therefore, when He moves, love moves. When He speaks, love speaks.

The love of God is not merely a feeling, but it is a divine force. When His Presence is in manifestation, divine love is the atmosphere that can be perceived by others.

If a man is to possess this divine love, he must first become a partaker of Eternal Life, the nature of God. This can only be done by becoming a child of God, being born again.

When Adam disobeyed God and sinned, the sin nature, the nature of the devil, came into him. He was no longer in fellowship with God, but was separated from Him; he became spiritually dead. With the fall of Adam, every man after that was born with a sin nature, separated from God; they were spiritually dead.

But Jesus came to bring Life (Eternal Life, the Life of God, the nature of God) to man, to restore him back to his rightful position that Adam lost. When Jesus paid the price for man's sin and defeated Satan, He made available to man the way back to God – to be restored back into fellowship with Him.

Romans 10:9 instructs us how to be born again. *"That if thou shalt CONFESS WITH THY MOUTH the Lord Jesus, and shalt BELIEVE IN THINE HEART that God hath raised him from the dead, thou shalt be saved."* When man confesses with his mouth that Jesus is Lord and believes in his heart that God raised Him from the dead, he is born again. Eternal Life comes into him. He is now a possessor of the Life and nature of God.

When man is born again, the Life of God, which is Eternal Life and the nature of God, comes into him, creating in him a new spirit. *"A new heart also will I give you, and a new spirit will I put within you: and I will take away the stony heart out of your flesh, and I will give you an heart of flesh"* (Ezek. 36:26). The old spirit that held death and the nature of the devil has been recreated; he has a new spirit that now contains Eternal Life and the nature of God.

"Therefore if any man be in Christ, he is a new creature: old things are passed away; behold, all things are become new" (2 Cor. 5:17). That old man has passed away and this

born again man has become a new creature in Christ, a new creation; that man becomes a new species of man that has never existed before.

This new creation, this new creature in Christ, is a love child of a love God. He is born again of love. He is now like his Heavenly Father; he now has the same nature – a love nature. *"...Every one that loveth is born of God, and knoweth God"* (1 John 4:7). You can't love with divine love unless you're born again.

That love nature has the ability to produce love thoughts, love words, and love actions. God can only manifest Himself through love, so that man now possesses the nature that God can flow through and manifest Himself through – a love nature.

Divine love is the very opposite of human love. It is not based on the flesh, feelings, emotions, temporal things, and temporal settings, but it is an outflow of the divine love that resides within the spirit of a born again man. This love is not born out of a physical or an emotional place. It doesn't spring from the reasonings of man, but from the spirit. This divine love is a strong starter and a strong finisher. It endures everything; it won't give up and quit. It won't abandon people, obligations, and responsibilities – it's not a quitter. It will never weaken and fail, no matter what pressures show up, for it never gives up. This divine love has no hate for others; it will never strike back in anger, fling words of hurt and hate at others, nor fight to get its own way or put itself first, for it's not selfish. This love turns homes and lives into love zones. This divine love will endure to the end. It stands up under any pressure without faltering or quitting – it stays true. It is without flaw.

This divine love is resident in every man that is born again – it came into him at the new birth. Romans 5:5 tells us, *"...the love of God is shed abroad in our hearts by the Holy Ghost which is given unto us."* We don't need to pray and ask for this love, for it is already resident in us since we now have God's nature, which is a love nature. We are to yield to it and allow it to dominate us.

Love is a fruit that resides in our spirit that came in us at the new birth (Gal. 5:22). Fruit grows. As our knowledge and understanding of the love God has for us grows, it will enable us to walk free from anything that is not born of love – fear, worry, doubt, and all things that seek to oppose us.

As we choose to yield and respond to it, that fruit of love will grow; it will flow out, blessing others and putting us over. It is the evidence that God is in us. *"By this shall all men know that ye are my disciples, if ye have love one to another"* (John 13:35).

Chapter 2

Know & Believe the Love

Of all the New Testament writers, John the Apostle seemed to express one of the greatest revelations of the love of God in his writings. (He wrote the Gospel of John, 1 John, 2 John, 3 John, and Revelation). He had such a revelation of God's love for him, that in several passages, he described himself as the one "whom Jesus loved." He made the love Jesus had for him his focus.

At the last supper, as Jesus spoke of the things that were to soon befall Him, John 13:23 describes the scene. *"Now there was leaning on Jesus' bosom one of his disciples, whom Jesus loved."* (We know this to be John, for that's how he described himself in his writings.) John *believed* the love Jesus had for him – so much so, that as a grown man, he reclined himself on this One. Even moments before His impending arrest and betrayal, the love and peace Jesus exuded was so complete and undisturbed that it seemed to be an invitation for John to recline on Him. There's no evidence that Jesus invited John into that position; John took it. It was a position any one of the twelve could have taken, but only one man did. He reclined on Love itself.

John writes, *"And we have KNOWN and BELIEVED the love that God hath to us..."* (1 John 4:16).

The Amplified Classic translation reads, *"And we KNOW (understand, recognize, ARE CONSCIOUS OF, by observation and by experience) and BELIEVE (adhere to and put faith in and rely on) the love God cherishes for us...."*

"And we have KNOWN...the love...." When did we "know" the love? We came to know it when the divine love of God came into us at the new birth – it is the love nature of God we now possess. As the Amplified Classic translation states, we are to be "conscious of" that love nature within so that we yield to it and allow it to dominate us.

We also come to "know" the love God demonstrates to us through experiencing all that love provided – salvation, healing, provision, peace, joy, victory, and all of God's blessings.

"...And BELIEVED the love that God hath to us...." The Amplified Classic translation reads, *"...BELIEVE (adhere to and PUT FAITH IN and RELY ON) the love God cherishes for us...."* We can "put faith in and rely on" the love God holds for us, for it will never run out, cease, or give up on us. We can count on it.

We "believe the love" in two ways – by believing the love God holds for each of us, and also by believing and laying hold of what love provided for us in Christ.

Love's Plan

Love is something you do; you can't love without giving. So, love made a plan. In God's great love plan for man, the Bible tells us that Jesus was as a Lamb slain from the foundation of the world (Rev. 13:8). His sacrifice was planned before the world was created. God's love for us was so great and so far-reaching that He provided for us before this world even came into being. *"For God SO LOVED the world, that he gave his only begotten Son..."* (John 3:16). Love compelled Him. Jesus was love's gift to the world. Jesus was proof of God's love for man.

God's love is the grandest and greatest thing in the world. God's love is the reason for man. Love wanted a family, and we are love children of the love God.

As the Creator of all things, His great joy and satisfaction come from giving of all He has to His love children.

Blessed With "All Things"

Love provided for man's need. By giving Jesus, love paid the price for the redemption of man. Love's price restored man back to right fellowship with God, imparted the Life and nature of God into man, made man the dwelling place of God, provided for every need of man, and has prepared an eternal home for him.

"He that spared not his own Son, but delivered him up FOR US ALL, how shall he not WITH HIM ALSO FREELY GIVE US ALL THINGS?" (Rom. 8:32).

Look at this phrase, *"...WITH HIM also freely give us ALL THINGS?"* Along with the gift of Jesus, God also gave us "all things." Connected to this gift of Jesus is "all things" we will ever need to live the life God authored for us. "All things" are given to us in Christ.

"For God SO LOVED the world, that he gave his only begotten Son...." It is God's love that gave us Christ, and it is that same love that provided "all things" in Christ – righteousness, health, prosperity, supply, victory, peace, etc., – all things.

God IS love; He can't cease being love, for that's what He is. Therefore, "all things" that love provided are as enduring as the Giver Himself; they will never run out or cease. Our righteousness, health, prosperity, supply, victory, peace, etc., will never cease.

How this convinces us of His great love for us! We "believe the love" that God has for us.

Love provided for every need of man in salvation: Eternal Life, righteousness, healing, prosperity, deliverance, victory, and all the blessings of God in Christ. To "believe the love" is to believe what love has provided for us.

To "believe the love" is to believe we are healed by Jesus' stripes, for that's what love provided for us. To "believe the love" is to believe the Word that tells us that God is our

Provider (Phil. 4:19); we believe that Jesus was made poor that we might be rich (2 Cor. 8:9). To "believe the love" is to believe what His Word tells us about all that He has done and provided for us.

Don't Believe Anything Contrary to Love

Don't believe anything contrary to the love! Walking in love includes refusing to allow any of these things love provided to be stolen from us. Don't give up anything love provided and made yours.

The devil attacks, tempts, threatens, lies, deceives, steals, kills, destroys, and seeks to work many ills against us, but we refuse to *believe* any of those things – we refuse to yield to any of it. Those things are all *takers* – love is a *giver*. We "believe the love" and what love provided!

Release your faith in His love for you by believing, speaking, and acting on what His love provided. To confess His Word over your situation is one way you "believe the love."

To "believe the love" God has for you includes putting your attention on God and His Word and refusing to be condemned, deceived, or enticed away by fear, worry, doubt, threats, distractions, feelings, circumstances, or any strategy and device of the enemy.

Romans 8:1 tells us, *"There is therefore now no condemnation to them which are in Christ Jesus...."* God doesn't condemn us with our sins or our past; He is the One who cleanses us from it with the Blood of Jesus.

When a woman caught in the act of adultery was brought to Jesus, He was silent in front of her accusers. When the accusers walked away, He asked her, *"...Woman, where are those thine accusers? hath no man condemned thee? She said, No man, Lord. And Jesus said unto her, NEITHER DO I CONDEMN THEE: GO, AND SIN NO MORE"* (John 8:10 & 11).

God never condemns us. The Word tells us that the enemy is the accuser of the brethren.

When we have a hunger and desire to please God, the enemy will try to take advantage of our sincerity to be pleasing to God and accuse us of failing Him. He will point to our faults, failures, and shortcomings and try to make us think that we have failed God and that God is mad at us. God isn't mad at us – He's our Helper.

To "believe the love" is to believe God and His Word, not the enemy and circumstances.

Colossians 2:15 tells us, *"And having spoiled principalities and powers, he made a shew of them openly, triumphing over them in it* (the Cross)." Jesus did that for us. He utterly defeated Satan on our behalf, then handed us the victory.

We don't fight the devil, but we enforce our victory over him. We remind him that Jesus already defeated him, and we refuse to allow anything that comes from the enemy to trouble or harass us. We take our stand against him, we resist the devil, and he flees from us. In every encounter with him, we are to always remember him as a defeated foe!

Love made us victors! Love won the battle for us! Love made us more than conquerors!

In His great love, He has provided victory for us over all the works of the enemy. Jesus declared, *"Behold, I give unto YOU power to tread on serpents and scorpions, and over all the power of the enemy: and nothing shall by any means hurt you"* (Luke 10:19). The power and authority that Jesus delegated to us is more than enough to overcome every enemy. When we exercise our authority, we are exercising what love won for us.

To believe anything Satan brings against us is to fail to "believe the love" God has for us. To believe what fear says to us is to fail to "believe the love" God has for us. To worry is to forget His love for us.

Don't believe anything more than you believe what God says! Don't believe anything more than you "believe the love" and what love provided.

Realize that attacks come to try to hinder, slow, or stop your spiritual progress. The enemy doesn't want you to come into the knowledge of the Word. He doesn't want you to gain light of the Word of God and what love made yours, for the light you gain and walk in enforces his defeat.

"And the light shineth in darkness; and the darkness comprehended it not" (John 1:5). Darkness doesn't have the ability to overcome or defeat light. Take your bold stand

against anything that tries to hinder you, put you down, or slow your progress. Walk in the light of love, walk in the knowledge of what love made yours. Satan is defeated, and love made you his master.

Believing Means To Act

Believing is an act! To "believe the love" doesn't mean to passively sit back and wait for God to do something because He loves you, but it means to act on what love already won and provided for you – act on the Word. Confess and act on what the Word says is yours; speak and act as one who is free, healed, provided for, and delivered. To be skillful with the love of God is to be skillful toward what love provided, laying hold of all things by faith.

It's wrong thinking that sits idly back and says, "Whatever will be, will be. Everything that happens is God's will. God won't let anything bad happen to me because He loves me." Yes, God does love us, but because He does, Jesus restored back to us our authority over the devil that Adam lost. We are the ones responsible to take a bold stand against the devil and resist him, forbidding him to work in our lives. Love won back the authority that we are to exercise.

To "believe the love" is to act on what love made ours by speaking the Word and resisting the devil who tries to steal God's blessings from us.

Love has made you Satan's master; he is your subject.

As you "believe the love" and act on what love provided and made yours, you are master! You are master in the realm of love and life.

Hold Fast

To "believe the love" involves *holding fast* to what love provided in the face of opposition. Love is a divine force, and it works whether we feel it or not. Even when we don't feel anything lovely, we don't wait to have a warm, fuzzy feeling before we "believe the love." We have faith and "believe the love" because of what the Word tells us that love provided, not because of what we may or may not feel.

Chapter 3

The Love Realm

[The Father] has delivered and drawn us to Himself out of the control and the dominion of darkness and has transferred us into the kingdom of the Son of His love, In Whom we have our redemption through His blood, [which means] the forgiveness of our sins.

— Colossians 1:13 & 14 (AMPC)

At the new birth, we changed kingdoms. No longer are we under the rule of Satan's kingdom; he no longer has rule over us – we have a new Lord. Love redeemed us. Love purchased man back from the kingdom of darkness and from the grasp of sin and translated us into the love kingdom. God translated us into the kingdom of the Son of His love; we are now under His rule and Lordship. We are citizens and love subjects of that kingdom – the love kingdom. As children of God, the love of God is now IN us, and that same love is the flow of God's kingdom.

We are citizens and love subjects of the love kingdom that produces all good things. Every good thing is the flow of that kingdom. *"...How beautiful are the feet of them that preach the gospel of peace, and bring glad tidings of GOOD THINGS!"* (Rom. 10:15).

Anything that is not good is not of love and doesn't come from God's realm; therefore, it doesn't belong to God's people and is to be rejected.

Every earthly king has a realm where his authority reaches. That which is under his authority is his royal jurisdiction and domain; it is his realm.

God has a realm, and His realm is the love realm; the law governing that realm is love. Jesus introduced that law when He stated, *"A NEW COMMANDMENT I give unto you, THAT YE LOVE one another; as I have loved you, that ye also love one another. By this shall all men know that ye are my disciples, if ye have love one to another"* (John 13:34 & 35).

We are to allow the love that is in our spirits to dominate and govern us. It is to be the governing law and flow of all we say and do.

Not only is the law of God's realm the law of love, but it is also the law of the New Covenant (New Testament) and is to govern the new creature (the believer).

When we yield to and respond to the divine love that is within us, we are responding to God and His realm; this keeps us safe from the enemy.

To yield to and respond to anything that is not love is to yield to a different realm than God's; this opens the door to the devil. Outside the realm of love is where Satan is functioning.

Paul warns us, *"Neither give place to the devil"* (Eph. 4:27). One of the primary ways we give place to the devil or open the door to him is by stepping out of love, leaving the love realm. That's how we end up on the devil's territory, and when we do, then he has a right to attack us.

My spiritual father often stated, "One step out of love is a step into sin." To step out of love is to step out of God's realm. Our safety lies with staying in God's realm, the love realm and the love kingdom.

As citizens of this love kingdom, we are to think, speak, and act in line with love, and we are to forbid anything that is not of God's realm to gain entrance into our lives.

Only someone with a love nature can function in this love kingdom, in the realm of love. The born again man now has that love nature; thereby, he can function, produce, and move in line with the love kingdom and the love realm; he is now a co-laborer with love, moving with God, moving with love. *"For in him we live, and move, and have our being..."* (Acts 17:28).

How this love nature elevates and brings dignity to man!

Revelation 1:6 tells us, *"And hath made us KINGS and PRIESTS unto God and his Father...."*

James 2:8 instructs us, *"If ye fulfil the ROYAL LAW according to the scripture, Thou shalt LOVE thy neighbour as thyself, ye do well."*

We have been made unto Him kings and priests, and love is the royal law of God's realm, God's kingdom; it is the flow befitting royalty and the royal place we now occupy. As kings and priests unto Him, this royal law is to govern us.

Chapter 4

Filled With God

Paul records what he prayed for God's people in Ephesians.

EPHESIANS 3:17-19
17 That Christ may dwell in your hearts by faith; that ye, being rooted and grounded in love,
18 May be able to comprehend with all saints what is the breadth, and length, and depth, and height;
19 And to know the love of Christ, which passeth knowledge, that ye might be filled with all the fullness of God.

The AMPC translation of verse 19 reads,

[That you may really come] to know [practically, through experience for yourselves] the love of Christ, which far surpasses mere knowledge [without experience]; that you may be filled [through all your being] unto all the fullness of God [may have the richest measure of the divine Presence, and become a body wholly filled and flooded with God Himself]!

This is what God planned that our lives should look like – that we would be filled through all our being (spirit, soul, and body) unto all the fullness of God, that we would have the richest measure of the divine Presence, and that we would become a body wholly filled and flooded with God Himself.

Think of what He is offering us – to be filled and flooded with God! Think of what this kind of life looks like. Think of what this kind of life produces. The devil fears this man. Darkness has no entrance into this man. This man is full of God and full of all that is good. When full, there is no room for anything else that is not of God.

Stephen's Fullness

Acts 6:8 tells of Stephen: *"And Stephen, FULL of faith and power, did great wonders and miracles among the people."*

The next chapter, Acts 7, tells how the religious leaders opposed and contended against him and took him outside the city to stone him. As they were stoning him, Acts 7:55 tells us, *"But he, FULL of the Holy Spirit and controlled by Him, gazed into heaven and saw the glory (the splendor and majesty) of God, and Jesus standing at God's right hand"* (AMPC).

No one else saw that day what Stephen saw. He saw the glory of God. He saw Jesus standing at God's right hand – what a view! Why did he see that? One reason – he was full! Those who are full of God will see things that others don't see – glorious things!

One man told his account of going to Heaven. He said that he got to speak with Stephen. In the course of their conversation, the man said to Stephen, "I read of how you were stoned. That must have been a painful death."

Stephen answered, "No, I never felt a thing because I was caught up in the glory!"

Again, remember that Stephen saw the glory because he was full. Being "wholly filled and flooded with God Himself" will remove us from things this natural world feels. It shields us from the hardness of tests and trials. Our fullness removes us from the flow of this world and brings us into the flow of glory.

This place of fullness is available to each of us to occupy. This fullness is God's love plan for His children.

Fullness Shielded Me

When my husband unexpectedly went home to be with the Lord, the Spirit of God had told me two years prior that all I was to do was "practice peace." So, I did. Any thought that didn't lead to peace, I resisted, refusing to touch it in my thought life and turn it over in my mind.

I did as God instructed us in 2 Corinthians 10:5. *"CASTING DOWN imaginations, and every high thing that exalteth itself against the knowledge of God, and bringing into captivity EVERY THOUGHT to the obedience of Christ."*

any thought that doesnt lead to peace. Resist refuse to touch it in my thought life & turn it over in my mind fullness places us outside the reach of the Devil. fullness leaves the enemy no room

So good

As a result, I moved into a place of the Spirit and into a fullness of God where peace was the governing flow.

At the report of my husband's homegoing, death was no match for the all-conquering force of peace – that peace shielded me from grief and sorrow entering in. I refused to touch thoughts of worry, fear, or grief, but rather, I focused on worshipping God – my attention was there and on Him.

I didn't try to fight against grief and sorrow entering in; rather, I focused on staying full of God. In that fullness, there was no room for grief and sorrow to enter, and I was held in peace; the fullness of God shielded me.

Fullness places us outside the reach of the devil. Oh yes, he will attack, but in the fullness, we fail to notice him, for our attention is on God. The fullness leaves the enemy no room.

Take Your Place

It is no wonder that Paul prayed as he did for God's people, "*... that you may be filled [through all your being] unto all the fullness of God [may have the richest measure of the divine Presence, and become a body wholly filled and flooded with God Himself]!*"

As one minister wrote:

> *I am convinced that the intelligent children of God could walk in the same life, power, and*

We are called to walk in the fullness of Divine life (life + nature of God dominating us)

Jesus will lead us into the full dream ambitions + purposes of our father!

divine liberty as Jesus walked, if they understood their privileges.

Walk in the realm of Life. I believe that God planned that we should walk in the fullness of Divine Life (with the life and nature of God dominating us); that we should dare to take our positions as sons and daughters of God; and the hour is coming before the Lord's return in which a remnant of the Body will rise and walk before God in the FULLNESS of the New Creation Life.

Disease will not be able to lay hold upon us.

Ignorance and fear will be banished, because the Wisdom that comes from above that is in Jesus will lead us into the full dream, ambitions, and purposes of our Father.

Faith will lead us where reason cannot walk. Reason has never been a mountain climber. Faith, like a mountain sheep, can scale the loftiest mountain peaks without fear.

Don't you think it is time that we passed out of the swaddling clothes period into the stature of the perfect man in Christ Jesus?

Let us dare to climb the heights of God.

Let us say without fear, "I am what He says I am. He is in me what He says He is. I can do with

*His ability in me what He says I can." This makes
life big and rich. This makes us worthwhile to
Him. We will be in that prized inner-circle with
Him, one of the trusted ones.*

*When He has a difficult mission, He will call
on us. You see, He will find it easy to reach us as
we constantly visit with Him.*

Take your place! Enjoy your rights!

[handwritten margin note: good]

[handwritten margin note: To work in, Complete Fullness of God]

Love & Fullness

Notice again how Ephesians reads.

EPHESIANS 3:17 & 18
**17 That Christ may dwell in your hearts by faith;
that ye, BEING ROOTED AND GROUNDED IN
LOVE,
18 May be able to comprehend with all saints
what is the breadth, and length, and depth, and
height.**

The NIV translation reads, that you *"...may have power
...to grasp how wide and long and high and deep is the love
of Christ."*

No matter how far away or how far down someone may
go, they are never outside the reach of God's love.

In verse 19, Paul continues to write, *"And to KNOW THE
LOVE of Christ, which passeth knowledge, that ye might
be FILLED with all the Fullness of God."* I want you to see

When we forbid entrance to the wrong things, then we are free to be filled with fullness of God.

that being filled with all the fullness of God is connected to knowing the love of God.

In the love of God, there is no guilt, accusation, condemnation, fear, dread, shame, grasping, poor self-image, frustrations with self, disappointment with self, or anything that puts you down. God never uses any of these things toward His children. All of these things are from the devil, and when these things try to trouble our mind, we are to resist them.

How do we resist them? By *answering* them with the Word. James 4:7 instructs us, *"...Resist the devil [stand firm against him], and he will flee from you"* (AMPC).

Yielding to wrong things hinders our fullness. Instead, we are to yield to the flow of love. When we forbid entrance to wrong things, then we are free to be filled with the fullness of God.

As we renew our minds to what love provided for us, we become rooted and grounded in love. To be filled and flooded with God Himself includes having lives that are filled and flooded with all that God provided for us in Christ.

What's Your Attention On?

I love a testimony I heard. This minister had been lamenting their own faults, flaws, and weaknesses and was feeling pushed down under them; it was hindering their spiritual progress.

It matters what our attention is on!

While considering these things, they had a vision of Jesus standing off at a distance in a desert. In between this minister and Jesus were many clear boxes scattered between them. Jesus said, "These boxes represent your faults, flaws, and weaknesses. If you look at them, they will trip you up. Just look at Me, and I will navigate you past them."

It matters what our attention is on.

A Vision of the Blood

My husband told of an experience he once had. While ministering in a church, there had been many healings in one of his evening services. When he returned to his hotel room that night, his mind began to be bombarded with thoughts like, *You shouldn't have said this, and you shouldn't have said that! You sure messed up your words tonight! You made so many mistakes!* The longer those thoughts bombarded him, the more discouraged he became toward himself and the service, even though many people had been helped. (One strategy of the enemy is to bring an attack after there has been a victory.)

The next morning, while shaving, those thoughts kept troubling his mind, and tears were running down his face. All of a sudden, he saw a vision. In the vision, he saw a bust of himself, then he saw a large hammer strike the top of that bust and cracks appear all over it. Jesus spoke to him, "Those cracks are all your weaknesses, faults, and flaws."

Any flow we yield to other than love will deplete and compromise our fullness. But the more we yield to & recieve of the love & God has for us, the greater the degree of fullness we will experience

"Yes, I know. I have so many," he continued to cry.

But all at once, in the vision he saw blood begin to flow into those cracks and fill them in, and Jesus said, "My Blood cleanses you of all your weaknesses, faults, and flaws."

Accuser of the Brethren

Satan is the accuser of the brethren. He accuses people with their past, faults, flaws, failures, shortcomings, and anything else that puts them down. But God never does! Love never does! Love has no part in that.

We are to "believe the love." That's the only way to experience fullness. If we believe wrong things against ourselves or against others, we compromise fullness.

Any flow we yield to other than love will deplete and compromise our fullness. But the more we yield to and receive of the love God has for us, the greater the degree of fullness we will experience.

As we walk in the light of the Word by being a doer of it and resist the accusations of the enemy, we are walking in the flow of love, and we close the door to those wrong things that try to put us down and hold us back.

We must learn to recognize the strategies of the enemy and take a stand against them, refusing to let them in. Then we are free to be "filled with all the fullness of God."

What's possible for the person who is filled & flooded with God!

Trying To Hinder Fullness

I remember in times past, when I would have feelings of discouragement and frustration with myself, I felt like I was failing God. Those feelings seemed to follow and bombard me; they would leave me grasping and frustrated with myself. As a result, I would find myself stepping back spiritually. Those accusations against me would seem to step in between me and my fellowship with God, causing me to draw back.

Once I recognized those feelings as an attack of the enemy and resisted them, that overwhelming feeling of failure would leave, and my fellowship with God would again flourish.

I realized it was all designed to hinder my spiritual progress, to hinder me from gaining greater revelation of the Word, and to hinder my spiritual fullness.

The enemy seeks to interrupt and affect our fellowship with God by drawing us into the mental and natural arenas and out of the spirit arena – which is the place of fullness – for he knows what is possible to the one who is full of God.

God-Inside Minded

Just think of all that is possible for the person who is "filled and flooded with God Himself." They enter in and live in the realm where all things are possible. There are no impossibilities to that man, that congregation, the Body of Christ – the filled ones!

The Doddridge translation reads, *"...I wish you more enlarged apprehensions of it* (the love of Christ), *that so ye may be filled with all the fullness of God, that your EXPANDED HEARTS, being DILATED more and more, may be rendered CAPABLE OF ADMITTING LARGER DEGREES THAN EVER OF DIVINE LOVE, and more ample indwellings of divine consolation, till at length ye arrive at that happy state in which ye shall attain to a full perfection in the knowledge and ENJOYMENT OF GOD..."* (Eph. 3:19).

The "enjoyment of God." I love that! He is our great joy! One of the greatest benefits of living full of God is the on-going experience of the "enjoyment of God."

The above translation states that as we have a greater apprehension of His love for us and all that His love provided for us, our hearts (our spirits) are enlarged to receive even greater degrees of divine love, filling and flooding us with God Himself.

To be filled and flooded with God Himself is to be God-inside minded to the full! With our thoughts and words full of His greatness and power, fullness is our flow.

To live full of God would include living mindful of His love that is within and yielding to its flow with love thoughts, love words, and love acts – always asking ourselves, *"What would love do?"*

Chapter 5

Perfect Love Casts Out Fear

*There is no fear in love; but perfect love casteth
out fear: because fear hath torment. He that feareth
is not made perfect in love.*

— 1 John 4:18

"There is no fear in love...." There is no fear in God, and
God has no dealings with fear. No fear comes from Him, and
He is not dealing with His children on the basis of fear. All
fear is from the enemy. Outside the realm of love is where
Satan and fear function. To stay in the flow of love is to stay
in the flow where no fear resides.

1 JOHN 4:16 & 17 (AMPC)
**16 ...God is love, and he who dwells and
continues in love dwells and continues in God,
and God dwells and continues in him.**
**17 IN THIS [UNION AND COMMUNION WITH
HIM] LOVE IS BROUGHT TO COMPLETION
AND ATTAINS PERFECTION WITH US....**

To develop in love, walk in constant fellowship w/God Walk in obedience to the word, choose to only think, speak & Act in line w/love. Recognize Anything that is not love & refuse to give place to it.

46   *Love: The Great Quest*

The one who walks in love has constant fellowship with the Father. In our "union and communion with Him," we become full and controlled by the love nature and character of God. In that fullness, we live lives of love – we only think, speak, and act in line with love, shutting out all other flows. As a result, fear has no room to enter or reside – fear is cast out.

"...PERFECT love casteth out fear...." "Perfect love" is a love that is developed and matured. To develop in love, walk in constant fellowship with the Father, walk in obedience to the Word, and choose to only think, speak, and act in line with love. We recognize anything that is not of love, and we refuse to give place to it – we refuse to think, speak, or act in line with anything that isn't love; we refuse to move in line with fear. As a result, fear is not given a place; fear is run out. Love casts out fear by only permitting love thoughts, speaking love words, and taking love actions. When only love is yielded to and permitted, there's no room for fear.

"...Fear hath TORMENT...." Fear attacks the mental arena, for the mind is Satan's battleground. When fear comes, it seeks to torment, trouble, and harass the mind. Anything that troubles and unsettles the mind is to be cast down.

When fear threatens, we must do as Paul instructed, *"Casting down imaginations, and every high thing that exalteth itself against the knowledge of God, and bringing into captivity every thought to the obedience of Christ"* (2 Cor. 10:5). Answer thoughts of fear with the Word. Tell fear what God said; tell fear what love said.

love is the flow where the mind is peaceful
refuse to touch fear in my thought life

Love is the flow where the mind is peaceful. So anything that threatens the peace that love made yours, (1) answer it with the Word and refuse to touch it in your thought life, (2) command fear to leave, (3) then take time to worship God, which helps hold your attention on Him. Believe the love that made victory yours.

Permit no troubling thoughts into your mind. And any troubling thought you have allowed in the past, run it out. Love offers you a mind of peace and soundness; it's part of your rights in Christ.

"...He that feareth is not made perfect in love." If your mind is troubled by fear, which can manifest as worry, depression, oppression, panic, anxiety, and any like things, the scripture prescribes your remedy – be made perfect or develop in love. To do that, fill up with the Word, renew your mind to the love God holds for you and what His love provided for you in Christ. Exercise your authority over fear, commanding it to leave you, then spend time worshipping God. Take your place in what love made yours.

The more we renew our mind to the truth of who we are in Christ and what belongs to us, the more easily we will recognize and resist fear. As we gain more light of how much God loves us and how much He provided for us in Christ, the more full we become of God and His love. The more we become skillful in love – receiving and yielding to that love, responding to and acting on what love made ours – that fullness shuts fear out. Fear has no room to reside and has no place of entrance into our life.

Established in Righteousness

Isaiah 54:14 instructs us: *"In righteousness shalt thou be established: thou shalt be far from oppression; for thou shalt not fear: and from terror; for it shall not come near thee."*

Jesus has made us righteous, which means to be in right-standing with God. We aren't righteous because WE did everything right, but because JESUS did everything right. Righteousness is not a feeling – it is our position. He made us righteous. That is what love did for us.

"In righteousness shalt thou be ESTABLISHED...." How are we established in righteousness? By renewing our mind to the truth that love made us righteous. We renew our mind and are established in the righteousness that is ours when we find out who we are in Christ.

Feed and meditate on scriptures that tell you who you are in Christ. Confess, "I am who the Word says I am. I have what the Word says I have. And I can do what the Word says I can do."

As we take our place in who Christ made us to be, we become established, firm, deep rooted, and anchored in righteousness. Then when winds of adversity blow, they cannot move us into oppression, fear, or terror because we are established in the righteousness that love made ours.

Those who are established in righteousness will have a clearer view of all that love has provided.

"In righteousness shalt thou be established: thou shalt be FAR FROM OPPRESSION; for thou shalt NOT FEAR: and (FAR) FROM TERROR; for it shall not come near thee."

Those established in righteousness will be FAR from oppression, fear, and terror, for those things can't reach righteousness; they have no access to righteousness. As we are established in our righteousness, we are outside their reach.

Oppression, fear, and terror are not to be "nipping at your heels" as you live; they are not to cloud and shadow your life. They are to be FAR from you. And they will be, as you establish yourself in (build in you) the truth that Jesus made you righteous – that's what love did for you!

Chapter 6

Correction: A Flow of Love

There are many flows to God's love – salvation, healing, prosperity, deliverance, victory, and all the blessings of God. But we can't overlook one very important flow of God's love in our life, and that is correction.

Proverbs 3:11 & 12 tells us, *"My son, despise not the chastening of the Lord; neither be weary of his correction: For WHOM THE LORD LOVETH HE CORRECTETH; even as a father the son in whom he delighteth."*

Correction is a flow of God's love for us. It is another way He shows His love for us, for He doesn't want us to miss out on His best.

Hebrews 12:9 states, *"...We have had fathers of our flesh which corrected us, and we gave them reverence: shall we not much rather be in subjection unto the Father of spirits, and live?"*

Instead of becoming stiff-necked or offended at His correction, we should be grateful. It is a manifestation of His love, and it's one way He protects and keeps us safe and helps us to receive and fulfill His best for our life.

However, we must be clear on how God corrects. He doesn't correct us by causing bad and evil things to happen to us. When something bad happens, we may learn something from it, but that isn't God's way of correcting and teaching us.

People in the world accuse God of all kinds of evil – of causing natural disasters, sicknesses and diseases, deaths of loved ones, tragedies, etc. – but God isn't the One causing or using any of these things to teach or correct people. Anything that steals, kills, and destroys is from the enemy (John 10:10).

God's way of correcting and teaching us is through the instruction of His Word.

Proverbs 21:11 reads, *"When the scoffer is punished, the fool gets a lesson in being wise; but men of [godly] Wisdom and good sense LEARN BY BEING INSTRUCTED"* (AMPC). When people scoff at and don't listen to instruction, they get into trouble; they learn their lesson the hard way. But a wise person will listen to instruction and avoid trouble; they learn the easy way.

> **PROVERBS 8:33 & 34 (AMPC)**
> **33 HEAR instruction and be wise, and DO NOT REFUSE OR NEGLECT IT.**
> **34 Blessed (happy, fortunate, to be envied) is the man who LISTENS to me....**
>
> **PROVERBS 9:8 & 9 (AMPC)**
> **8 Reprove not a scorner, lest he hate you; reprove a wise man, and he will love you.**
> **9 Give instruction to a wise man and he will be yet wiser; teach a righteous man (one upright**

**and in right standing with God) and he will
increase in learning.**

**PROVERBS 19:20 (AMPC)
20 Hear counsel, receive instruction, and
ACCEPT CORRECTION, that you may be wise
in the time to come.**

To receive the instruction and correction God gives through His Word will bring us into His wisdom and will bring increase into our life.

It matters how we respond to His correction. We are to accept the responsibility of any wrongdoing, rather than try to shift it from ourselves and onto another, and be quick to repent and to make changes.

Such joy comes from acting on 1 John 1:9. *"If we confess our sins, he is faithful and just to forgive us our sins, and to cleanse us from all unrighteousness."* As we act on this verse, we are cleansed, and our fellowship with God can continue to flourish.

The Amplified Classic translation reads, *"If we [freely] admit that we have sinned and confess our sins, He is faithful and just (true to His own nature and promises) and will forgive our sins [dismiss our lawlessness] and [continuously] cleanse us from all unrighteousness [everything not in conformity to His will in purpose, thought, and action]."*

To repent doesn't show a man to be weak, rather, it shows his strength. It's weakness that shifts blame, but it takes a strong man to acknowledge his sin and wrongdoing and to make a change. God can bless that man.

To repent means to make a change. We have the help of the Greater One on the inside to empower and assist us in making needed changes; we are to draw on His help and respond to Him by letting our spirit dominate and govern us.

2 CORINTHIANS 3:18
But we all, with open face beholding as in a glass the glory of the Lord, are CHANGED into the same image from GLORY TO GLORY, even as by the Spirit of the Lord.

Change brings us into greater degrees of glory. In His love for us, God corrects us because He wants to bring us into greater degrees of glory. As we receive the correction He gives and make any needed changes, greater glory is the result.

To receive correction God gives is to walk in love toward God.

SECTION 2
OUR LOVE FOR GOD

Chapter 7

"If a Man Love Me..."

And thou shalt love the Lord thy God with ALL THY HEART, and with ALL THY SOUL, and with ALL THY MIND, and with ALL THY STRENGTH: this is the first commandment.

And the second is like, namely this, Thou shalt love thy neighbour as thyself. There is none other commandment greater than these.

— Mark 12:30 & 31

Our love for God is to involve our whole being. To love Him as we ought calls for all our heart, soul, mind, and strength. We don't just give Him our heart, but our all is His. He is not only our Savior, but He is to be the Lord of our life. And as Lord, He will want to have something to say about how we live, where we go, and the company we keep. Nothing of us is to be reserved or held back from Him.

"We love him, because he FIRST loved us" (1 John 4:19).

Because He loved us first, that love compelled Him to provide redemption's plan. And in that plan, Eternal Life is made available to all men; however, it must be received. *"But as many as RECEIVED HIM, to them gave he power to BECOME THE SONS OF GOD..."* (John 1:12).

To those who receive Him, Eternal Life comes into their spirit, which is the Life and nature of God Himself indwelling man. This is the new birth. At the new birth, man becomes a partaker of the nature of God, which is the love nature that comes into man. Now man can live and love on God's level and in God's realm. He is no longer bound and held captive to the natural, carnal, flesh-ruled realm of man, but man is now translated and lifted into God's realm – the love realm. Because man is a partaker of the Life and love of God, he now loves with God's own love – divine love. He is no longer living by the limits of natural, human love.

Because God first loved us, love provided all this for man. In response to His love, we now love God and others with that divine love. *"We love him, because he first loved us."* Now we can reciprocate with divine love back to Him. We love Him for first loving us, even when we were lost and unlovely!

The Abode of God

Not only did Jesus introduce and demonstrate the Father and the Father's love for man, but He also made a way for us to have access into the Father's Presence, as well as become a habitation of God.

Jesus declares, *"Behold, I stand at the door, and knock: if any man hear my voice, and open the door, I will come in to him, and will sup with him, and he with me"* (Rev. 3:20). As we hear, open the door, and are willing to sup with Him, He will come in and sup with us.

> **JOHN 14:21-24**
> **21 He that hath my commandments, and keepeth them, he it is that LOVETH me: and he that loveth me shall be loved of my Father, and I will love him, and will MANIFEST myself to him.**
> **22 Judas saith unto him, not Iscariot, Lord, how is it that thou wilt manifest thyself unto us, and not unto the world?**
> **23 Jesus answered and said unto him, If a man LOVE me, he will KEEP MY WORDS: AND MY FATHER WILL LOVE HIM, AND WE WILL COME UNTO HIM, AND MAKE OUR ABODE WITH HIM.**
> **24 He that loveth me not keepeth not my sayings: and the word which ye hear is not mine, but the Father's which sent me.**

"...We will come unto him, and MAKE OUR ABODE WITH HIM" (vs. 23). What a high honor this bestows on man!

The Father, Jesus, and the Holy Spirit make their abode with the man who loves Him and keeps His Word, for where He is loved and obeyed, He is welcomed and feels at home.

The atmosphere of every home reflects its residents. Where God abides, His Presence will bring great provision to that place – health, joy, peace, and great blessings. He meets the needs of the home where He abides; it is a safe, joyful place.

"I Will Manifest Myself to Him"

The previous passage reads, *"He that hath my commandments, and keepeth them, he it is that loveth me: and he that loveth me shall be loved of my Father, and I will love him, and will MANIFEST myself to him"* (vs. 21).

How will He manifest Himself to us? First, He will unveil Himself in the Word to the one who loves Him. Second, as doers of His Word, His Word will produce fruit in our life that will be visible to us and others. Thirdly, as doers of His Word, our life will be filled with the Presence of God.

Keeping His Commandments

Verse 21 also tells us, *"He that hath my commandments, and KEEPETH THEM, he it is that loveth me...."* We can SAY we love God and Jesus, but over and over the Word states that the one who loves God is the one who KEEPS His Word. To love God is to love His Word and to keep it, for He and His Word are one.

We say with the Psalmist, *"O how LOVE I thy law (Word)! It is my meditation all the day"* (Ps. 119:97).

It's not enough to be acquainted with the Word, to carry it around, or even to be able to repeat it. But it is the doer of the Word that demonstrates his love for God. When the Word is given its place in our daily life, directing and dominating our thoughts, words, and actions, our love for God is demonstrated and becomes visible to Him and others.

If we say we love Him, our thoughts, words, and actions must reveal that – we must be doers of His Word.

"But be ye DOERS of the word, and NOT HEARERS ONLY, DECEIVING your own selves" (James 1:22). We only deceive ourselves when we say we love Him, but our thoughts, words, and actions don't depict that. As our love for Him grows, so does our "doing" of the Word. In our love for Him, we give Him His rightful place in our daily life.

Chapter 8

Love & Obedience

Deuteronomy 30:20 instructs us, *"That thou mayest LOVE the Lord thy God, and that thou mayest OBEY his voice, and that thou mayest CLEAVE unto him: for he is thy life, and the length of thy days...."*

Loving the Lord and obeying Him are forever linked together. To love Him is to obey Him, and to obey Him is to love Him.

The one who loves and obeys Him "cleaves" or holds fast to Him, and their fellowship with Him flourishes.

This verse also tells us that in their love and obedience, He is their life and the One who enables them to fulfill all their days on this earth.

DEUTERONOMY 28:1 & 2
1 And it shall come to pass, if thou shalt HEARKEN DILIGENTLY unto the voice of the Lord thy God, to observe and to DO all his commandments which I command thee this day, that the Lord thy God will SET THEE ON HIGH ABOVE ALL nations of the earth:

2 And all these blessings shall come on thee, and overtake thee, if thou shalt hearken unto the voice of the Lord thy God.

There is a place at the top for us, but we must meet the condition – do all that He commands – we must obey His Word and His plan for our lives. We must obey His written Word and also obey what He speaks to us by His Spirit. The blessing is in the obedience.

Jesus stated, *"If ye keep my commandments, ye shall ABIDE in my love; even as I have kept my Father's commandments, and abide in his love"* (John 15:10). Jesus lets us know that He did abide in His Father's love by keeping His commandments. And that's how we are going to continue to abide in Jesus' love – by keeping His commandments.

To love the Lord is to love the Word, for God and His Word are one.

Walking in Love Toward God

First John 5:3 tells us, *"For this is the LOVE OF GOD, that we KEEP HIS COMMANDMENTS: and His commandments are not grievous."* We are to be mindful of walking in love toward others, but let us not forget that we are to walk in love toward God, too. How do we walk in love toward God? By keeping His commandments – obeying His Word.

If we fail to walk in love toward others, our faith won't work, for faith worketh by love (Gal. 5:6). But if we fail to walk in love toward God, our faith won't work either.

Obedience is a flow of our love toward God. Obeying God holds us in the love flow, and then we will get results with our faith.

My spiritual father used to say, "If I get sick, the first place I check is my love walk." He would check there first to see if he had opened the door to the devil. One step outside of love is a step into sin; and when you're in sin, you're on the devil's territory, and then he has a right to attack you.

Well, when we check our love walk, let's not only check our love walk toward men, but also toward God. Are we walking in love toward Him? Are we keeping His commandments? Are we obeying what He told us to do – either through His Word or by His Spirit?

"I Delight To Do Your Will"

"For this is the love of God, that we keep his command-ments: and HIS COMMANDMENTS ARE NOT GRIEV-OUS." So much of the time, we struggle and struggle against something God tells us to do or calls us to. But I have found that at those times, when I finally obey, I realize that strug-gling against it was far worse than just obeying.

The enemy will attack you in an arena you are called to. He wants you to set your will against God's will and against what God has planned for you.

During the 1980s, when I first traveled overseas with my husband to minister, there came such an attack on me that

I didn't want to do any more overseas travel. Afterwards, I seldom traveled with my husband overseas.

However, during one prayer service I was conducting at our church, Jesus walked up on the platform and stood by my chair. He instructed me, "I want you to travel overseas with your husband." So, from then on, I again went with him. And I'm so grateful I did because when my husband went home to be with the Lord, the doors to those other countries were still open to me to minister there.

I realized that the enemy had attacked me in that arena because overseas travel is part of the will of God for my life.

Now, when preparing to travel overseas, if the enemy tries to trouble me, I answer him, "No, you don't! I delight to do God's will (Ps. 40:8). His will is never grievous to me." Then I start thanking and worshipping God for the privilege to minister overseas.

As I renewed my mind with the Word regarding God's will, the devil could no longer gain entrance to trouble me about that.

Psalm 40:8 reads, *"I delight to do Your will, O my God; yes, Your law* (Word) *is within my heart"* (AMPC). Notice that when the Word is abiding in our heart, we will be delighted to do the will of God. If struggling with something of God's will for your life, feed and act on the Word regarding obedience until your mind is further renewed with His Word and abiding in your heart.

Now, when I arrive in another country, I worship God, saying, "I'm so glad to be home! Father, Your will is my home! So I am perfectly at home in this place!"

We are to refuse to allow the flesh, the world, or the devil to get us to set our will against God's will. We must never complain or speak against God's will for our life – that's dangerous. It is our great joy, privilege, and honor to carry out God's will for our life.

We are to consecrate ourselves to His will – bringing our will into agreement with His.

Jesus declared, *"My meat is to do the will of him that sent me, and to finish his work"* (John 4:34). The Amplified Classic translation reads, *"...My food (nourishment) is to do the will (pleasure) of Him Who sent Me and to accomplish and completely finish His work."*

Jesus let us know that as food nourished and sustained His body, the will of God nourished and sustained His life.

Years ago, God spoke to me and said, "Make My people to know that long life is connected to My plan." To veer from His plan is to veer from long life. We must prize and value His plan for our life above all else. For as we live out His plan for our life, we live the best life, and our life bears much fruit.

As Isaiah 1:19 reads, *"If you are WILLING and OBEDIENT, you shall eat the good of the land"* (AMPC). God not only wants us to be obedient, but He wants us to obey with a right attitude; He wants us to obey Him willingly.

When my children were young, it not only mattered to me that they obeyed what I instructed them to do, but that they did it with a right heart and a right attitude. Even if they obeyed, they could still get in trouble if their attitude was all wrong.

Well, God wants the same thing of His children. He wants us to obey, but He wants us to obey willingly – with a right heart and a right attitude.

God has done so much for us that we are to be grateful to do anything He commands us to do with joy, for His commands are not grievous. We are to be delighted to do His will.

I love the definition for holiness that one faith pioneer gave. "Holiness is doing the will of God with joy."

God's plan is that we eat the good of the land – that we experience and possess the best things in life. That can only happen if we are willing and obedient to His plan for our life.

PHILIPPIANS 2:13
For it is God which worketh in you both to WILL and to DO (obey) **of his good pleasure.**

(AMPC)
[Not in your own strength] for it is God Who is all the while effectually at work in you [energizing and creating in you the power and desire], both to WILL and to WORK for His good pleasure and satisfaction and delight.

The enemy wants you to struggle against God's plan for your life, trying to get you to set your will against God's will. But instead, learn to confess this verse in Philippians 2:13 over yourself. Also, renew your mind with the Word, saying, "I delight to do God's will. It is not grievous to me. It is my joy and honor to fulfill His will for my life!"

As we obey God, we demonstrate our love for Him, and we remain in the flow of love. *"If ye keep my commandments, ye shall ABIDE in my love...."*

Love focuses on obeying God. God's will and plan for our life is great, and obeying His will and plan brings us into that greatness.

SECTION 3
LOVE IN US

Chapter 9

Growing in Love

We are born of love. We are love children of a love God, and we belong to the love kingdom and the love realm. It is His own love which He has given us to conduct our life of love and His love business on the earth. But it is our responsibility and privilege to develop that love He has made ours so that it dominates and governs us. That love is under our stewardship to see to it that it develops and grows strong.

"But the fruit of the Spirit is LOVE, joy, peace, longsuffering, gentleness, goodness, faith, meekness, temperance: against such there is no law" (Gal. 5:22 & 23).

These fruits that are listed came in us at the new birth. They are not simply emotions or feelings, but they are forces – forces that will overcome and safeguard us from all opposition. Therefore, we need to cultivate them, causing them to grow and develop, and yield to them. As we do, they will enable us to live the life God authored for us.

Cultivating the Fruit of Love

Love is a fruit of the spirit, and just as the fruit on a tree grows, the fruit that resides in our spirit needs to grow.

But for love to grow, develop, and produce sweet fruit, it must be tended to and cultivated. It must be watered with the Word. Also, we must guard the fruit of love, protecting it from the weeds of offense, unforgiveness, and bitterness, and all unlovely things, for they will choke out and rob from the growth of love.

That love grows and develops as we feed on the Word of God, as we fellowship with God in prayer, and as we walk in love. As we renew our minds with the Word, then we grow to think like God thinks, and we allow that love to dominate our thoughts, words, and actions. At all difficult times and places in life, we should ask ourselves, "What would love do?"

As love is fed on in the Word and nurtured in God's Presence, we must yield to it, allowing it to dominate and govern our daily life.

Second Corinthians 5:14 instructs us that, *"...The love of Christ CONSTRAINETH us...."* The Amplified Classic translation reads, *"For the love of Christ CONTROLS and urges and impels us...."*

When the natural mind and the flesh of man want to respond in a way that isn't love, that love in our spirit will constrain us. It will help us control our flesh. Although that love constrains us, we must yield to it and not override it.

JUDE 1:20 & 21 (AMPC)
20 But you, beloved, BUILD YOURSELVES UP [founded] on your most holy faith [make progress, rise like an edifice higher and higher],

PRAYING IN THE HOLY SPIRIT (in other tongues)**; 21 GUARD AND KEEP YOURSELVES IN THE LOVE OF GOD....**

As we take time to pray in other tongues, not only will we be building or charging ourselves up on our most holy faith, but we will also be guarding and keeping ourselves in the love of God.

Love Constrains Us

Before my husband was born again, he was in construction work. One co-worker would invite him to church all the time, but my husband would become irritated and decline with some very colorful language.

Finally, my husband asked him, "Alright, if I go to church with you one time, will you leave me alone about going?"

"Yes," his co-worker agreed.

"Alright, I will go with you this Sunday." Ed kept his word and attended with him, and he was born again.

After being born again, Ed asked his co-worker, "Is there something physically wrong with you?"

"No," he answered, "why do you ask?"

"Before I was born again, you would go to the restroom a lot."

"Yes," the co-worker said, "when I would invite you to church and you would cuss me out, I would get so angry with you that I would go to the restroom and pray in tongues to keep from hurting you!"

This man tapped into a very important truth. When tempted to say or do something outside of love, by taking the time to pray in other tongues, he yielded to his spirit where love resided, and the love in him rose up and constrained him; it helped him keep his tongue and flesh under control.

If you find yourself in a situation that tempts your tongue, stay quiet and step back. Go to a place where you can be alone and take time to pray in other tongues. As you yield to that love within, it will constrain you from saying or doing something outside of love.

Practice this in your marriage, with relatives, on the job, and in any difficult situation. It will make all the difference.

Practice yielding to the love within that constrains you. The more you overstep it, the less sensitive you will become to it, but the more you yield to it, the more sensitive you will become to it.

Love Made Perfect

1 JOHN 4:16-19
16 And we have known and believed the love that God hath to us. God is love; and HE THAT DWELLETH IN LOVE DWELLETH IN GOD, AND GOD IN HIM. 17 Herein is OUR LOVE MADE PERFECT, that we may have boldness in the day of judgment:

because as he is, so are we in this world.
18 There is no fear in love; but PERFECT LOVE
casteth out fear: because fear hath torment. He
that feareth is not MADE PERFECT IN LOVE.
19 We love him, because he first loved us.

(AMPC)
16 And we know (understand, recognize, are conscious of, by observation and by experience) and
believe (adhere to and put faith in and rely on) the
love God cherishes for us. God is love, and he who
dwells and continues in love dwells and continues in God, and God dwells and continues in him.
17 IN THIS [UNION AND COMMUNION WITH
HIM] LOVE IS BROUGHT TO COMPLETION
AND ATTAINS PERFECTION WITH US, that
we may have confidence for the day of judgment [with assurance and boldness to face
Him], because as He is, so are we in this world.
18 There is no fear in love [dread does not ex-
ist], but FULL-GROWN (COMPLETE, PER-
FECT) LOVE turns fear out of doors and ex-
pels every trace of terror! For fear brings
with it the thought of punishment, and [so]
he who is afraid has not reached the FULL
MATURITY OF LOVE [is not yet GROWN
INTO LOVE'S COMPLETE PERFECTION].
19 We love Him, because He first loved us.

Through our union and communion with God, the divine
love within us grows and matures, and we are "made perfect"
in love. The one who has ongoing fellowship with the Father
walks in love. And the one who walks in love has ongoing

fellowship with the Father. He becomes full and possessed of the very nature and character of God.

As we practice love daily, we make every person and circumstance our practice ground. Love dominates and governs us, and we become skillful and masterful in the love realm. And it is true of us, *"...as He is, even so are we in this world."*

Chapter 10

Love & Faith

...Though I have ALL FAITH, so that I could remove mountains, and have not charity (LOVE)*, I AM nothing.*

– 1 Corinthians 13:2

It's interesting to note the last three words of this verse say, *"...I am nothing."* It doesn't say, I HAVE nothing, it says, *"...I AM nothing."* It's love that makes us "something." It's love that gives life its greatest value and importance.

The Amplified Classic translation reads, *"...If I have [sufficient] faith so that I can remove mountains, but have not love (GOD'S LOVE IN ME) I am nothing (a USELESS NOBODY)."*

It's love that makes us a "somebody." It's God's love in us that makes all the difference in the life we live.

Love is to be the compelling force behind all that we think, say, and do. Thank God for faith, for without it, we cannot be pleasing to God (Heb. 11:6). But without love, even "all faith" is as nothing, for faith can never take the place of love. Faith is no substitute for the lack of love. When love is absent, faith cannot make up the difference. We can't just throw more faith at a situation where love is called for and expect to get results.

We should grow and develop our faith by feeding on God's Word so that our faith becomes robust, for it is by our faith that we are able to conduct business with Heaven. But in developing our faith, we must also develop and grow in our love and our love walk.

The Greatness of Love

"And so faith, hope, love abide....these three; but the GREATEST of these is LOVE" (1 Cor. 13:13, AMPC). Faith, hope, and love are all great, powerful forces, but love is the greatest force of them all.

Many are looking to achieve greatness in life, but for the one who develops their love walk and is dominated by it, they live a life of greatness – love ushers them into the flow of greatness. Love is the greatness. It is the greatest force available to man.

Where love is absent, greatness cannot reside, no matter what natural, human achievements are accomplished. In this temporal, natural realm, human achievements may be admired and applauded, but without divine love they will fade away with time; they will not endure, for they only reside in this temporal world.

But this divine love flowing from within the believer is the outflow of the Life and nature of God Himself. This divine love within is a force that will abide and endure throughout eternity. So great is this divine love that any thought, word, or deed born of and motivated by this love will be rewarded and last through eternity. Love and what love produces will not die or end with this temporal world. The greatness of love will be seen in this temporal realm, but more importantly, it will endure in the realm of eternity. Divine love affects both realms – the natural and the spiritual realm.

Faith Works by Love

Galatians 5:6 tells us that faith works by love. Love is the fuel to faith. Faith is a great force, but without love, it goes nowhere.

Faith is important, and our faith must be in good working order, for it's by faith that we receive all that God has provided and conduct business with Heaven. But if we want to be a receiver, we have to be a lover, too. For when we stop walking in love, our faith stops working.

My oldest son, Stephen, stated, "You can load a train full of goods, but if that train isn't on the track, those goods aren't going anywhere. Love is the train track to move those goods into your life." Yes, faith works by love. When love is missing, the train is off the track. It doesn't matter how many wonderful items are on that train – without love those items never arrive.

"...This is the victory that overcometh the world, even our faith." If it's in the world, faith can whip it, faith can overcome it. Our faith is the victory. The greater the faith, the greater the victory. Our victory is waiting for our faith to show up. But our faith can only show up when love is in place.

My daughter-in-law, Morgan, stated the following:

> *"By this we know that we love the children of God, when we love God, and keep his commandments. For this is the love of God, that we keep his commandments: and his commandments are not grievous. For whatsoever is born of God overcometh the world: and this is the victory that overcometh the world, even our faith"* (1 John 5:2-4).

Faith is Heaven's currency. If we have been living carnal, it will keep our faith account low, and then we will have difficulty making a faith withdrawal. We must make deposits into our faith account every day.

But before talking about our faith that overcomes the world, John first tells us to love God and keep His commandments and to love the brethren.

A strong love life protects our faith life. Our love life protects our faith account. Strong robust faith must be protected by a strong love life. Love is the protection and security system for the household of faith.

EPHESIANS 3:17-19
17 That Christ may dwell in your hearts by faith; THAT YE, BEING ROOTED AND GROUNDED IN LOVE,
18 May be able to comprehend with all saints what is the breadth, and length, and depth, and height;
19 And to know the love of Christ, which passeth knowledge, that ye might be filled with all the fullness of God.

"...Rooted and grounded in love...." As my son, Stephen, stated, "Everything you build must have a foundation under it to stand. Faith needs a foundation – love is the foundation that faith must be built on if it is to stand."

Our foundation must be guarded and protected against damage and erosion, for without that sound foundation, the life we're building is compromised and in jeopardy. As the Word says, it's the little foxes that spoil the vine (Song of Solomon 2:15). It's the little things that can easily go undetected, or reach down to the foundation, doing their damage. Don't allow faith's foundation of love to be compromised through unforgiveness, offense, ill will, or anything else outside of love's flow.

Chapter 11

Love & Forgiveness

And Jesus answering saith unto them, Have faith in God.

For verily I say unto you, That whosoever shall say unto this mountain, Be thou removed, and be thou cast into the sea; and shall not doubt in his heart, but shall believe that those things which he saith shall come to pass; he shall have whatsoever he saith.

Therefore I say unto you, What things soever ye desire, when ye pray, believe that ye receive them, and ye shall have them.

And when ye stand praying, forgive, if ye have ought against any: that your Father also which is in heaven may forgive you your trespasses.

But if ye do not forgive, neither will your Father which is in heaven forgive your trespasses.

– Mark 11:22-26

In verse 22, Jesus tells us to have faith in God, (the original reads, "Have the faith OF God"). In verse 23, He then tells us that faith speaks to obstacles in our way; talk to things, and they will obey you. In verse 24, He tells us how to have our desires met. In verse 25, He lets us know one of the primary things that will keep our faith from working – unforgiveness.

To walk in forgiveness is an act of love. Love forgives. To fail to forgive is to step out of love, and when we aren't in love, we open the door to the enemy to attack us.

Forgiving others keeps us on safe territory, love's territory.

Forgiveness is a decision – it's not a feeling; it's a choice we make. We are able to forgive, for the love of God is in us, and it's with that love that we forgive.

We are to choose to forgive, whether we feel forgiveness or not; it's a choice of our will.

We forgive with words, not with feelings, so it doesn't matter how we feel.

When someone has wronged us, we simply say, "Father, Your love is in me, so the power to forgive is in me, so I forgive them, in Jesus' Name."

If someone has wronged you, don't wait until they repent before forgiving them. What if they never repent? We forgive them anyway, because we forgive based on the love that is in us, and not based on them and whether they ever treat us right.

When you forgive them, it does more for you than it does for them. It keeps you from being held captive by unforgiveness. By forgiving, you stay on love's territory, and your faith can continue working; we need our faith in good working order all the time.

Luke 23:33 & 34 reads, *"And when they were come to the place, which is called Calvary, there they crucified him...Then said Jesus, Father, forgive them; for they know not what they do...."*

Those who operate outside of love really have no idea what they're doing. If they really understood the danger of operating outside of love, they wouldn't choose to go there.

Choose to forgive before anyone ever does you wrong. That way, you aren't left to make your choice at the time someone wrongs you – you've already made your choice.

Forgive & Forget

When we forgive, we also forget, for that's what forgiveness does; that's how God forgives us – He forgives and forgets, never to bring it up again.

If the memory of what someone did comes back, answer it. Tell it, "I have forgiven them, therefore, I have forgotten it, and I refuse to remember it." Then cast those memories down, refusing them entrance into your thought life (2 Cor. 10:5).

Since we choose to forgive and forget, that means that we don't remind anyone else of what they did wrong either. We don't try to put them down or control them with anything of their past.

If feelings of unforgiveness try to come, answer them the same way. We don't walk by feelings. Forgiveness isn't a feeling – it's a choice we make. Don't allow feelings to make your choice for you – let love choose.

In the passage above, Jesus stated, *"And when ye stand praying, forgive, if ye have ought against ANY..."* (verse 25). You are included in that word "any." You must not only forgive others, but you must also forgive yourself if your faith is to work.

In 1 John 1:9 we are told, *"If we confess our sins, he is faithful and just to forgive us our sins, and to cleanse us from all unrighteousness."*

Once we confess our sins, God forgives us and forgets it, whether we feel forgiven or not. Once we confess it, we are to thank Him for forgiving us and cleansing us from all unrighteousness. We must release our faith in this verse, regardless of what we feel.

Hebrews 9:14 tells us, *"How much more shall the blood of Christ...purge* (cleanse and make clean) *your conscience from dead works to serve the living God?"*

The Blood of Jesus cleanses your conscience from the dead works of sin. One translation reads, *"So how much more will his blood wash from our minds our feelings of guilt for committing sin!"* One Greek commentary stated, "How much more shall the Blood of Jesus purge the 'replay of the mind' from dead works."

Once we confess our sin to God, the Blood of Jesus cleanses us, and we are not to permit any "replay of the mind" that condemns us or brings shame. Answer any troubling thoughts, saying, "No, the Blood of Jesus cleanses me and my mind, and I won't accept them." Then refuse to touch those thoughts in your thought life.

We must make sure we don't allow any unforgiveness toward others or toward ourselves, for we need our faith to work.

Chapter 12

Love & Healing

My spiritual father stated, "I count more on my love walk to keep me healed than I do on my confession of faith." He knew that stepping outside of love was an open door to sickness.

Yes, faith matters, but it only works and gets results when walking in love. All the healing confessions in the world won't override a lack of walking in love. Faith is not meant to take the place of love. Faith has its role – and it's an important role – but it is no substitute for love.

If we receive healing through someone else praying for us or ministering to us, it will be up to us to exercise our faith so we can *maintain* it and not lose it. But our faith will only work as long as we are walking in love. We must walk in love, as well as faith, if we are to *maintain* what we have received from the Lord.

The devil is busy trying to steal from us everything that God ever blessed us with, including healing. So when we receive healing, the devil will launch a counterattack to try to steal it from us. We must hold fast to what we receive and refuse to allow it to be stolen from us. To hold fast, we must exercise our faith, and we must believe what love provided for us, but we must also walk in love, for our faith only works by love (Gal. 5:6).

My spiritual father told of the time that God spoke to him to warn a minister. This particular minister was on the forefront in the Body of Christ. He had a powerful healing and miracle ministry, and multitudes flocked to his services. The results of his healing ministry were notable and dramatic. But God told my spiritual father to warn him of three things: his diet, his handling of money, and his love walk toward other ministers and the brethren.

The minister did not judge himself, and he died in his late 30s. Although he had a ministry that was on the forefront and had a powerful anointing, none of that could substitute for the lack of love. Not operating in love was an open door to the devil to attack him with sickness.

It's good and it's right to serve God, as this minister did, but all that we do for God is no substitute for the lack of walking in love.

We must walk in love with all people and not become combative in any of our relationships – in our marriage, with relatives, on the job, or with anyone else. My husband stated, "If you've got a fighting spirit, always fighting others, it will catch up with you – you will have physical problems."

The commandment of love is a spiritual law that cannot be violated, omitted, or overlooked – it is to govern us. Our life and health depend on it.

The Criteria

PHILIPPIANS 4:8
Finally, brethren, whatsoever things are true, whatsoever things are honest, whatsoever things are just, whatsoever things are pure, whatsoever things are lovely, whatsoever things are of good report; if there be any virtue, and if there be any praise, think on these things.

Paul gives us a checklist of criteria that must be met before we allow something into our thought life and mouth. It must be: true, honest, just, pure, lovely, and of good report. A thought or word we speak must meet each of these requirements. It may be true, but if it's not lovely, we are to reject it. It must meet each criteria.

During a conversation, a minister told what they had heard a certain person say, which didn't show that person in a good light. When the minister said it, the Spirit of God said to them, "If you talk about others, you're going to get sick." What they said was true, but it wasn't lovely, therefore, it was a step out of love, which is an open door to sickness.

We are warned in 1 Peter 3:10, *"For he that will LOVE LIFE, and see GOOD DAYS, let him refrain his tongue from evil, and his lips that they speak no guile."*

A sick day isn't a good day. A broke day isn't a good day. A troubled day isn't a good day. If we are to "love life and see good days," we have to watch and guard what we do with our mouth.

Psalm 141:3 instructs us, *"Set a watch, O LORD, before my mouth; keep the door of my lips."* The Holy Spirit will help be a watch over our mouth, but we must not overstep and ignore Him when He checks us. The love within us will constrain us, but we must yield to that constraint and not overstep it.

Lay Your Hand on Your Mouth

Proverbs 30:32 warns us, *"...if you have thought evil, lay your hand upon your mouth"* (AMPC). We must catch a wrong thought and cast it down before it ever reaches the mouth, for once it's spoken, it is set in motion and opens the door to the devil.

Years ago, I was preparing for a very important event I was to speak at that week. There would be about 4,000 people present with many public officials and dignitaries in attendance. At the time, there was a flu epidemic that was widespread, and as I was preparing for the event, the devil said to me, "I'm going to make you sick." I recognized fear speaking, so I answered it back, "Oh no, you won't, because I'm the healed!" And I dismissed the thought.

The next night, I was preaching in our church during a midweek service. During my sermon, I was getting ready to make a statement that was derogatory about another denomination. Right in mid-sentence, the Holy Spirit gave me a strong check. I recognized it, but because I was in mid-sentence, I just finished my statement. I finished my sermon, then exited the sanctuary to go into our hospitality room. The moment I exited the sanctuary, every flu symptom came on me in full force in an instant. The symptoms didn't just gradually come, but they were all immediately on me. I recognized where I had missed it.

I gathered my things and then drove home; I felt so sick. As soon as I got in the house, I went to my kitchen table and sat down, and I prayed, "Okay, God. I disobeyed You. I recognized that Your Spirit checked me about the statement that I was getting ready to make, but because I was in mid-sentence, I said it anyway. I was wrong, and I repent. Now, I can't plead ignorance, because I knew Your Spirit tried to stop me. I don't ask You for justice, because I'm guilty; I did wrong. So, I plead mercy. I have to speak at this important event in the morning. I can't be sick. I must be there."

"Okay," God answered, "I will heal you, but on Sunday morning, you get up and repent to your congregation for what you said. If you don't, every flu symptom will come back on you at the end of the service."

"You have a deal!" I quickly agreed. "I will gladly do that!"

The moment I said that, the power of God struck me and every flu symptom was instantly gone. The next Sunday, I held up my end of the bargain. I repented to my congregation, and the flu never came back on me.

At the event I conducted, I gave a salvation call when I was finished speaking, and hundreds were born again. That's why the devil threatened me with sickness. He was trying to stop that great harvest of souls from coming in. But I was the one who had opened the door to him through saying something that wasn't born of love.

I thank God that His mercy met me, and because of it, I was healed. Thank God that His mercies are new every morning!

Don't Permit Unforgiveness

One believer told the testimony of his young son who had a tumor. When they took him to the doctor, the doctor was not very concerned about his condition and told him that it was just a very routine surgery to remove it. So, they had it removed. But to the doctor's surprise, the tumor grew back, so they again had it surgically removed. However, after a short time, the tumor grew back a third time.

The father of the boy was troubled as to why the tumor kept growing back. He had prayed for his son, but this time, he took a different approach in his praying. Instead of just praying for his healing, he asked God if there was an open door to the devil; if there was, he wanted to get that door closed so that his son could be healed.

As he prayed, God spoke to him, "You have never forgiven your own father." There had been some conflict in the past with his father, and since that time, he had carried that unforgiveness. When he realized where he had missed it, he asked for forgiveness and then forgave his father, letting his unforgiveness go. When he did, the tumor on his son disappeared.

When we step out of love, not only does that open the door to sickness on ourselves, but it can open the door on loved ones – on anyone and anything that is under our authority.

Walking in love not only protects us from sickness, but it will protect our children, our home, our business, and every arena of our life. Love is a security system on our life that we must not compromise. When walking in faith and love, no intruder can gain entrance to us or anything under our authority.

We thank God for the medical help that may be received when in need, but medical issues can continue if there is an open door to the devil through failure to walk in love.

Love Obeys

We are the custodian of our body. God may speak to us or deal with us about making a change in how we are handling our body. He may deal with us about our diet, about getting proper rest, or about exercise. In His love for us, He is trying to help us and protect our health.

We need to make sure that we are walking in obedience to anything that God has dealt with us to do. Obedience is a flow of our love toward God that will bless our own life.

Chapter 13

Love & Prosperity

Several years after starting our church in California, I had spent a few weeks teaching on prosperity. As I was preparing to again minister on that, the Spirit of God spoke to me, "You need to back up. Until you teach these people how to walk in love in their homes, they don't qualify for BIBLE PROSPERITY."

Notice the wording He used – "Bible prosperity." There is a measure of prosperity you can gain in the world just by hard work, but "Bible prosperity" is different – it involves our faith, and it has no sorrow attached to it. It comes by the blessing of the Lord.

"The blessing of the LORD, it maketh rich, and he addeth no sorrow with it" (Prov. 10:22).

When God prospers you, He doesn't have to steal from one arena of your life to increase you in a different arena. He won't steal from your marriage or your family life to increase your prosperity. He won't steal from your spiritual life or from your role in the local church to prosper you. He won't steal from your health to bring you into prosperity.

Those in the world who toil to become rich will have to rob from the other arenas of their life to have some prosperity. They will rob from their marriage and family life, and they will compromise their health and good health practices to prosper. As a result, there will be sorrow added into their prosperity. Many end up in divorce courts, have troubled children, and have broken health.

As believers, we want to make sure that we don't slip into the world's system of prosperity, but stay with God's system.

As we are doers of the Word and follow God's will and plan for our life, we position ourselves for Him to prosper and increase every arena of our life – our marriage, family, business, and health. God's will is our wealthy place – that's where all of God's best can be received. That's "Bible prosperity."

But notice what else the Spirit of God said to me. "...Until you teach these people how to walk in love in their homes, they don't QUALIFY for Bible prosperity."

Yes, whether we realize it or not, we must *qualify* to enjoy Bible prosperity. All the blessings of God are conditional. All He has provided for us doesn't flow automatically – there are qualifications – we must walk in faith, walk in love, and walk in obedience to God and His Word to receive what has been provided.

For example, the right to drive a vehicle belongs to all citizens. But we still have to *qualify* to drive in this nation.

We must complete a driving course, pass a written exam, pass a driving test, pay a vehicle registration, pay for and carry proof of vehicle insurance, have a vehicle that meets state requirements, and abide by the safety and driving laws. By meeting all these guidelines, we qualify to drive. Without qualifying, we cannot drive – we cannot take advantage of our right to drive.

Likewise, prosperity belongs to all of God's people, but it isn't automatic. No, we don't have to earn that blessing, but we must qualify.

The foremost way we qualify is by walking in love. Prosperity and all the blessings of God can only be activated and received in our lives by faith, but without love, our faith won't work. To prosper, our love must be in place, and our faith must be in good working order.

If we step out of love, the prosperity that belongs to us can't be received. God doesn't withhold prosperity from us, but if we aren't walking in love, we are out of position to *receive*, and the prosperity God gives won't reach us. If we want to be a *receiver,* we have to be a *lover,* for when we stop walking in love, our faith stops working.

When you own a cell phone, there are some conditions that must be met for that phone to work. You must have a service plan, and you must be within range to get a signal on your phone. Without a signal, the phone won't work. You have to get back into position for that phone to receive a signal if it is to work.

If you don't get a signal, your service is interrupted. You don't lose your phone, and you don't lose your service plan – they still belong to you. But you must position yourself so you can get a signal if you are to benefit from the phone and service plan that belong to you.

Walking in love positions us to *receive* the prosperity God made ours – it *qualifies* us to receive what God has already provided.

Strife Destroys Increase

The book of Acts reveals one of the enemies to increase, and that's strife.

> **ACTS 6:1-5**
> **1 And in those days, when the number of the disciples was multiplied, there arose a murmuring of the Grecians against the Hebrews, because their widows were neglected in the daily ministration.**
> **2 Then the twelve called the multitude of the disciples unto them, and said, It is not reason that we should leave the word of God, and serve tables.**
> **3 Wherefore, brethren, look ye out among you seven men of honest report, full of the Holy Ghost and wisdom, whom we may appoint over this business.**
> **4 But we will give ourselves continually to prayer, and to the ministry of the word.**
> **5 And the saying pleased the whole multitude....**

When the church was growing, strife arose, so the apostles immediately gave a solution that pleased the multitude. Verse 3 tell us the guidelines they put in place. The congregation was to appoint seven men with three qualifications: they had to be men of honest report, full of the Holy Ghost, and full of wisdom.

Men who are honest, full of the Holy Ghost, and full of wisdom are men who will not lend themselves to strife, but instead, they bring peace to volatile situations. Strife and division can come through carnal, natural men, but those who are spiritual yield to and produce unity and peace.

When these seven men were put in place, strife ended, unity returned, and increase continued.

Don't Permit Strife

Genesis 13 tells us that Abram was rich with gold, silver, and cattle, and his nephew, Lot, who was with him, had cattle. Their herds together were so great that the land couldn't support their need for food and water. So strife arose between those tending the herds for Abram and Lot.

In verses 8 & 9 Abram offers Lot a solution.

GENESIS 13:8 & 9
8   And Abram said unto Lot, LET THERE BE NO STRIFE, I pray thee, between me and thee, and between my herdmen and thy herdmen; for WE BE BRETHREN.

9   Is not the whole land before thee? separate thyself, I pray thee, from me: if thou wilt take the left hand, then I will go to the right; or if thou depart to the right hand, then I will go to the left.

Abram refused to engage in strife, so he offered Lot the first pick of the land. If Lot wanted the land to the right, Abram would go to the left. If Lot wanted the land to the left, Abram would go to the right. So, Lot chose for himself the best land in the direction of Sodom and Gomorrah.

Abram would not fight his nephew for the land – he wouldn't get into strife with a brother. Abram knew that the blessing was with him – not with the land. Wherever he went, the blessing went. He knew that the blessing would make any land bloom. There was no need to fight his brother.

God later changed Abram's name to Abraham, and he continued to flourish under the blessing of the Lord upon him.

To increase in the blessing of the Lord, you may have to do as Abram did and separate yourself from those who permit strife in their lives. When I say separate, I don't mean to become unkind and cut people off, but don't allow them a governing voice in your life; you may have to put distance between them and you. That is an act of love, for that protects peace.

We see no more conflicts arise between Abram and Lot. On a couple of occasions, Abram had to rescue Lot, but we have no record of them ever living together again. Abram separated himself from Lot, not out of offense, but to stay away from the strife that arose in Lot's life.

It's important to notice that Abram wouldn't fight his brother, Lot, for land, but when enemy kings attacked Sodom and Gomorrah, carrying Lot and his family into captivity, Abram pursued them with his own private army and got Lot and everything back; he carried away great spoils from the kings.

Abram wouldn't fight a brother, but when an enemy who wasn't a brother attacked, he completely defeated them (Gen. 14).

We don't fight a brother. Love not only walks in love toward the brethren, but love refuses to allow the enemy to steal from it!

Every Evil Work

Strife will destroy increase. When a marriage enters into strife, increase will stop flowing. No amount of prayer, giving, or confession of prosperity scriptures will make a difference until the strife is addressed.

In pastoring, I would often state to the congregation, "Before you enter into strife, ask yourself this question, 'Do I have enough money to fund this strife?' " When strife enters, increase is hindered, and no matter how much money someone may have, it's never enough to fund strife.

Not only does strife affect financial increase, but it can open the door to sickness on yourself or your loved ones.

James 3:16 warns us, *"For where envying and strife is, there is confusion and every evil work."* Strife gives "confusion and every evil work" an open door and unhindered access into your life and home.

So much of the time, strife arises due to money issues. Some will even allow their marriage or other relationships to break down over it. People will go to great lengths to protect their money, but we need to protect our love walk and our faith, also. We can always get more money, but the price of not walking in love costs us much.

When love is given its place in our life and in our home, strife ends. Love means the end of strife.

A Giving Nature

There is no need for a Christian to yield to strife, for the love of God on the inside offers us the highest way to live – a life of love.

Love turns you into a giver, for the nature of God in the believer is a nature of giving. *"For God so loved the world, that He GAVE His only begotten Son..."* (John 3:16). When we give, we are being true to the nature of God that is in us.

One way that love is expressed in this realm is through giving. We can't love without giving.

SECTION 4
OUR LOVE FOR OTHERS

Chapter 14

Love & the Home

A love home means the end of strife, quarreling, bitterness, and selfish words that harm and injure. It has a Heaven-like atmosphere; it's a place where children thrive and want to be.

In almost 30 years of marriage, my husband and I had Heaven on earth. That was possible because we were both renewing our mind with the Word of God and allowing the Word to dominate us.

One strategy of the enemy is to bring accusing thoughts against your spouse, pointing to their weaknesses, faults, and failures, but God won't. Love will recognize and cast down those thoughts, refusing to accept them.

When walking in love, you put the other person first. In our marriage, we put each other first; that way, we both got to be first. If we would have put ourselves first, we would have had to put the other one down to do that. Human love is selfish – it only does what benefits and suits itself, but divine love puts the other person first.

Love is generous. And generosity should be evident within a marriage and in the home. Anytime my husband heard me say that I liked or wanted something, he would make it his assignment to get it for me. Knowing this, I didn't take advantage of or manipulate his generosity.

To have a flow of love in the home, the tongue must be controlled. In the book of Jude, we see an instruction that benefits every life, marriage, and home. *"But ye, beloved, building up yourselves on your most holy faith, praying in the Holy Ghost, KEEP YOURSELVES IN THE LOVE OF GOD..."* (Jude 1:20 & 21).

We should take time to speak in tongues on a daily basis, for the benefits are immeasurable. When faced with difficulties or when in a conversation that tempts your tongue, stay quiet and step back. Go to a place where you can be alone and take time to pray in other tongues. As you do, you are yielding to your spirit where love resides, and that love within you will rise up and constrain you from saying or doing something outside of love; it will help keep your tongue and flesh under control. Love is not only saying the right thing, but leaving unsaid the wrong thing at the tempting moment. Keep yourself in the love of God; praying in the Holy Ghost plays a role in that. Practice this in your life, and especially in your marriage and home.

One way to make quick adjustments in your marriage and home is to consider what you would do if Jesus were physically in your home. How would you talk to Him? How would you treat Him? How would you serve Him? Consider that in how you treat your spouse. If you wouldn't think it, say it, or do it to Jesus, then don't think it, say it, or do it to your spouse or to anyone else. Treat your spouse the way you would seek to bless Jesus if He were physically in your home.

To have Heaven in your home, don't try to get your own way – go love's way.

Atmosphere of Love

While raising our children, we protected the atmosphere of our home. We didn't allow strife, yelling, and shouting at one another in the home. We didn't permit harsh words in our home.

As parents, we didn't use harsh words in correcting them. We corrected our children in a way that didn't push them down. We never told them that they were bad. We dealt with them if they did something bad, but we never made them feel like they were bad children.

When I was growing up, my mother never told us we were bad. When we misbehaved, she would say, "You're sweeter than that. But when you act wrong, no one knows how sweet you really are."

"We Will Serve the Lord"

I love what Joshua stated, "*...as for me and my house, we will serve the Lord"* (Josh. 24:15). He recognized that it was his responsibility to determine the direction of his household.

He didn't ask those in his household how they wanted to live; he was the one who determined how they would live and trained them in that way.

We don't ask our children if they want to attend school. We know it's right for them, so we make the right choice on their behalf, and we train them in that choice. Even so, we know that living in obedience to the Word is the right choice, so we make that right choice on their behalf, and we train them in that choice.

Proverbs 22:6 instructs us, *"Train up a child in the way he SHOULD go: and when he is old, he will not depart from it."*

One way a child *should* go is the way of love. Children must be trained in the way of love.

When I was young, I remember my mother correcting us if we complained against or talked negative about others. She would stop us and say, "That's a bad habit. Stop that!"

Criticizing, fault-finding, gossiping, or talking negative is a bad habit. Don't allow it to become a practice in the home for yourself or your children. It is the job of the parent to determine the direction of the household, to enforce the law of love in the home, and to not permit any to veer from it.

To talk about the faults, failures, and sins of others in front of your children will cause them to be critical and untrusting of others; it will injure their love walk and their spiritual life. Never allow anyone in your home to be critical of people, especially of those in the Body of Christ. Protect your home and the flow of love in the home by keeping those things out.

Chapter 15

Love & Ministry

The motive for ministry is one thing – love for people. It's love that compelled God to send Jesus, it's love that Jesus demonstrated throughout His earthly ministry, it's love that still compels Him as His ministry continues at the right hand of the Father, and it's His great love work that we are carrying on in the earth.

God said to me years ago, "I'll never send you to minister to someone you don't love." Love is the greatest qualification for ministry. We must love the lost so we can minister to them. We must love the unlovely so we can minister to them. We must love those who are bound so we can minister to them. We have what they need – God's love, God's Word, and God's power. The greater our love for people, the more God can use us.

We can't effectively minister to anyone we are critical of. The way we think and speak about others will affect how God can use us.

Speaking the Truth in Love

In ministering to others, we give them the Word, for it's the Word that will take a man's life and set it on course. Love lifts people up to the standard of the Word, for that's what offers them the best life.

The Word finds its greatest expression through us when we speak it in love.

Proverbs 16:21 tells us *"...the sweetness of the lips increaseth learning."*

Ephesians 4:15 instructs us, *"But SPEAKING THE TRUTH IN LOVE, MAY GROW UP INTO HIM in all things, which is the head, even Christ."*

As we teach the truth of God's Word in love, that's the setting people can grow in. The delivery makes all the difference. A sweet delivery of the Word of God helps it enter more easily into the listener. We are instructed to "speak the truth (the Word) in love." If it's not spoken in love, it's no longer the Word. Oh yes, the words may be the same, but if the tone, the motive, or the intent of the preacher isn't love, it no longer represents God and His Word.

When our sons were young, Grant delighted in making his older brother think that he was in trouble. On one particular occasion, I told Grant to tell Stephen that I wanted him. He wasn't in trouble, but I just needed him to do something for me. Grant went to the bottom of the stairway and yelled up to his brother in his most scary, intimidating voice, "Steeeephen, moooother wants YOOOOU!"

Grant said the same words I said, but he changed the tone and intent of the words to suit him – it was a harassing tone. Stephen came downstairs thinking that he was in trouble for sure! Grant had accomplished his mission, but not mine. He put his own spin on what I said.

Well, God doesn't want us putting the wrong spin on His Word. He tells us that we are to "speak the truth IN LOVE."

We aren't to deliver the Word of God in such a way that pushes people down, but rather lifts them up – we are to speak it in love. Matthew 12:20 tells us about Jesus, *"A bruised reed shall he not break...."* When someone who comes to Him is hurting, He helps them, He lifts them. When people come to church, they are asking for bread. We don't give them a stone – we don't scold, condemn, criticize, put down, accuse, or point to what they're not. We lift them! We tell them who God has made them to be. We let them know that God sees them with the eye of faith; He sees them "in Christ," and so do we. As we deliver the Word, people are helped, and people are to be lifted. That's love's way!

If we are going to live in divine health, we have to lift people up, not push them down.

Love & Power

The goal of life and of ministry must be love, not power.

When we look at 1 Corinthians, we see chapter 12 list the nine gifts of the Spirit, we see chapter 13 describe divine love, and then we read the following in chapter 14.

1 CORINTHIANS 14:1 (AMPC)
Eagerly pursue and seek to acquire [this]
love [make it your aim, your great quest]; and
earnestly desire and cultivate the spiritual
endowments (gifts)....

Notice that in this verse, love is spoken of before we are instructed to desire and cultivate ministry endowments or gifts. The local church and the people that are dominated and ruled by love are positioned properly for a flow of power. Spiritual gifts are displays of God's power, and we are instructed to "earnestly desire and cultivate" them in our churches; we are to gain knowledge and skill with them.

In 1 Corinthians are listed the nine gifts of the Spirit.

1 CORINTHIANS 12:8-10
8   For to one is given by the Spirit the word of
wisdom; to another the word of knowledge by
the same Spirit;
9   To another faith by the same Spirit; to
another the gifts of healing by the same Spirit;
10 To another the working of miracles; to
another prophecy; to another discerning of
spirits; to another divers kinds of tongues; to
another the interpretation of tongues.

These nine gifts only come into manifestation as the Spirit wills, not as we will. But when the Spirit wants to manifest Himself through these gifts, we must yield to and cooperate with Him. It takes faith to yield to the Spirit in flowing with these gifts, and if our faith is to work right, we must walk in love, for faith works by love. When faith and love are in place, the power of the Holy Spirit can flow through us unhindered.

Follow Love

In 1 Corinthians 14:1, we are instructed to, *"FOLLOW after charity* (love)*, and desire spiritual gifts...."*

When ministering, there are times when I see someone, and a strong sense of love rises up in me toward them. I recognize that love is drawing me toward them because God wants me to minister to them with a gift of the Spirit. When I follow that love and call them out, then God gives me clarity in what He wants ministered to them – a gift of the Spirit will go into operation for them.

Love Protects Us Against Pride

When we are grounded and developed in love, that keeps our motives pure and pleasing to the Lord, protecting us from pride.

We must guard against wanting to be used of the Lord with great displays of power just so we may be seen of men or to build our ministry. Motivation for ministering healing power to people is not about our ministry, but about our love for people.

Whenever someone is used of the Lord in a powerful way, know that the enemy will attack, and if love is not in place, the enemy will have an entrance. Having love as our only motivation protects and guards us from pride and keeps the door closed to the enemy.

Chapter 16

Love's Way

And we have known and BELIEVED THE LOVE that God hath to us. God is love; and he that dwelleth in love dwelleth in God, and God in him.

— 1 John 4:16

To "believe the love" includes believing that love is the highest and best way to walk. It is the way of God's realm. It is the commandment we live by; it governs our life.

Jesus loves every person who is bound by sin – He loves them enough to help them. That's where we come in. We are the love channels He will use to reach and help them. The only channel He can use is someone who loves them. It's our job to extend them the love that frees them and leave the rest with God. There is a world waiting for love to show up and rescue them. Because they don't always recognize what their rescue looks like, they may push it away, but we just keep extending love their direction – we don't give up.

Loving Our Enemies

We belong to God's family because someone didn't give up on us. God didn't give up on us. Love didn't give up on us.

Because His love is in us, we continue to follow that love, letting it lead us into love victories. Now that His love has found its home in us, it is for all, and we allow it to flow freely. We permit love to have its way in us. We don't withdraw the love that won us, but we freely keep extending it to others, letting it reach them. We are love channels to those who are lost, to fellow believers, to our loved ones, and to all people.

Love protects. When walking in love, we protect our family, those under our authority, and those in the Body of Christ, but we are not out trying to protect ourselves. In fact, love won't even take notice when others mistreat us; love chooses to ignore it.

We know we are taking our place in love and love is being given its rightful place in us when we seek not our own – we no longer put ourselves first – but others.

As my spiritual father said, "When someone opposes me, I just treat them like they bragged on me." How could he do that? He ignored it. He responded to them based on the love in him rather than based on them and their actions.

Jesus instructed us, *"But I say unto you, Love your enemies, bless them that curse you, do good to them that hate you, and pray for them which despitefully use you, and persecute you"* (Matt. 5:44).

In this verse, Jesus assigned love four things:

(1) love your enemies

(2) bless them that curse you

(3) do good to them that hate you

(4) pray for them which despitefully use you
     and persecute you

Love, bless, do good, and pray. This is how we treat our enemies and those who oppose us.

How are we able to do these things? When He tells us to love our enemies, along with the command, He gives us the love itself – it's His own love that has already been shed abroad in our hearts.

Psalms shows us how David responded to his enemies.

PSALM 35:11-14
11 False witnesses did rise up; they laid to my charge things that I knew not.
12 They rewarded me evil for good to the spoiling of my soul.
13 But as for me, when they were sick, my clothing was sackcloth: I humbled my soul with fasting; and my prayer returned into mine own bosom.
14 I behaved myself as though he had been my friend or brother: I bowed down heavily, as one that mourneth for his mother.

David was not glad when his enemies suffered. In love and sincerity, he prayed for them.

Proverbs 24:17 & 18 warns us, *"Rejoice not when thine enemy falleth, and let not thine heart be glad when he stumbleth: Lest the Lord see it, and it displease him...."*

Proverbs 16:7 tells us, *"When a man's WAYS PLEASE THE LORD, he maketh even his enemies to be at peace with him."*

What ways please the Lord? Love's ways. When our enemies oppose us, and our way of responding is to love, bless, do good, and pray for them, then the Lord can make our enemies to be at peace with us because we gave Him something to work with. When we respond in love, God can work with that. But if we respond with something other than love, then He can't work with that.

When we forgive, we forget – that's how God treats us. We don't recall someone's wrong so we can remind them of it and use it against them. No, we choose to forget it.

Choose Love

Corrie ten Boom and her family helped hide Jews from the Nazis in World War II. Her family was found out and was sent to a Nazi camp where they all died, except for Corrie. She and her sister had experienced many terrible things in those camps, including solitary confinement, hard forced labor, and physical abuse. Corrie watched her sister die in that camp.

Upon her release, she went everywhere preaching the Gospel. She would tell the people, "No matter how deep your darkness, God's love is deeper still."

After one of her services, a man came forward to greet her. He thanked her for her message and stated that upon hearing her preach the Gospel, he had received Jesus. As he spoke with her, she realized that he looked familiar, but she couldn't remember where she had seen him. Then, she remembered. He was the prison guard who had beaten her sister so severely.

As he stood there, thanking her for the message and telling her that he had received Jesus, Corrie struggled. She remembered how cruel he had been to her sister, and with those memories, she felt bitterness and resentment. But she prayed silently, "Jesus, help me to love this man." She didn't feel love for him, but she was willing to let love dominate her. All at once, as she yielded to that divine love, the love of God that was resident in her heart came flooding up, overriding all feelings of bitterness and resentment. With God's love and great joy, she forgave the man and rejoiced with him that he was now a brother in Christ.

Human love could not have done that, but divine love did. God not only tells us to love our enemies, but He also gives us His own love with which to love them. However, we must be willing to allow that love within to rise up and dominate us.

The Help of the Spirit

The enemy works through people to bring great hurt, harm, and injury to others, but this divine love is the remedy. Choosing to let His divine love within to dominate will make all the difference and will free those who have been wronged from all hurt and harm. We choose to forgive because we remember that we too have been forgiven.

"But ye, beloved, building up yourselves on your most holy faith, praying in the Holy Ghost, KEEP YOURSELVES IN THE LOVE OF GOD..." (Jude 1:20 & 21). One of the greatest benefits of praying in the Holy Ghost, in other tongues, is that the Holy Spirit will remove all hurt and harm caused by others and by hurtful situations. All we have to do is make the choice to forgive and forget, choosing to let it go, and He is the One who will remove it; it will seem as though the hurt never existed. We don't have to get rid of it, but we must choose to let it go, and He will fully remove it.

Luke also records what Jesus stated, but he records an additional statement. *"But love ye your enemies, and do good, and lend, hoping for nothing again; and YOUR REWARD SHALL BE GREAT, and ye shall be the children of the Highest..."* (Luke 6:35).

There is a reward for those who walk in love toward their enemies and toward those who oppose them – and it's a great reward!

Loving All

When we are unsure of what the proper response is to a situation, just stay on the side of love. As my spiritual father stated, "It's better to err on the side of love than on the side of sin."

As one evangelist stated, "It's God's job to judge, the Holy Spirit's job to convict, and my job to love."

"If ye fulfil the royal law according to the scripture, Thou shalt love thy neighbour as thyself, ye do well" (James 2:8). Who is our neighbor? Not just the one living next door to us, but the one standing next to us in line in the store, the one driving next to us down the road, the one working next to us in the office, as well as the one who lives next to us within our own home. Your neighbor is anyone you come in contact with. They are to be swept up into the love flow of your life.

The more Christ-like we are, the more conscious we are of others rather than ourselves.

> **1 JOHN 3:14-18**
> **14 We know that we have passed from death unto life, because we love the brethren. He that loveth not his brother abideth in death.**
> **15 Whosoever hateth his brother is a murderer: and ye know that no murderer hath eternal life abiding in him.**
> **16 Hereby perceive we the love of God, because he laid down his life for us: and we ought to lay down our lives for the brethren.**

17 But whoso hath this world's good, and seeth his brother have need, and shutteth up his bowels of compassion from him, how dwelleth the love of God in him? 18 My little children, let us not love in word, neither in tongue; but in deed and in truth.

"...He that loveth not his brother abideth in death. Whosoever hateth his brother is a murderer: and ye know that no murderer hath eternal life abiding in him." This passage tells us that to hate is the same as murder, as far as love is concerned. In divine love, there is no hate for anyone. If a believer says they hate someone, they don't really hate them, for the love of God is in them. They are just allowing their flesh to dominate them instead of that divine love within them. They have stepped out of the love realm and onto the devil's territory (and that's dangerous territory). Never allow any feelings of hate to override the love of God within. We reject feelings that are in opposition to love; instead, we allow love to dominate us. We forbid any thoughts or words of hate, rather, we choose to think and speak love.

Especially Toward the Household of Faith

It is such a great privilege to belong to God's family, and we are to demonstrate our love toward this great love family. Remember, love does something; love performs love acts.

GALATIANS 6:10 (AMPC)
So then, as occasion and opportunity open up to us, let us do good [morally] to all people

[not only being useful or profitable to them, but also doing what is for their spiritual good and advantage]. Be mindful to be a blessing, ESPECIALLY TO THOSE OF THE HOUSEHOLD OF FAITH [those who belong to God's family with you, the believers].

We are to walk in love toward all men, but this scripture shows us that it especially matters how we treat those in the Body of Christ. We are never to say or do anything that would harm a brother or the place the brethren gather, the local church, for then we are touching the Body of Christ, and it is dangerous to step out of love with our brethren. We are to only do good and bless our brethren, which is God's family.

JOHN 13:34 & 35
34 A new commandment I give unto you, That ye love one another; as I have loved you, that ye also love one another.
35 By this shall all men know that ye are my disciples, if ye have love one to another.

Jesus commands us in John 15:9, *"As the Father hath loved me, so have I loved you: CONTINUE ye in my love."* (We are to carry on the great love work He began. We are His love representatives in the earth.)

JOHN 15:10-13
10 If ye keep my commandments, ye shall abide in my love; even as I have kept my Father's commandments, and abide in his love.
11 These things have I spoken unto you, that my

joy might remain in you, and that your joy might be full.
12 This is my commandment, That ye love one another, as I have loved you.
13 GREATER LOVE HATH NO MAN THAN THIS, THAT A MAN LAY DOWN HIS LIFE FOR HIS FRIENDS.

Love makes sacrifices for the benefit of others – that's love's way.

Chapter 17

Love Defined

Though I speak with the tongues of men and of angels, and have not charity, I AM BECOME as sounding brass, or a tinkling cymbal.

And though I have the gift of prophecy, and understand all mysteries, and all knowledge; and though I have all faith, so that I could remove mountains, and have not charity, I AM NOTHING.

And though I bestow all my goods to feed the poor, and though I give my body to be burned, and have not charity, IT PROFITETH ME NOTHING.

– 1 Corinthians 13:1-3

This warns us that without love and without a motive of love, our lives miss the mark. This passage of scripture highlights spiritual acts that can look impressive to others – speaking in other tongues, prophesying, the understanding of all mysteries and all knowledge, faith that can remove mountains, giving all goods to feed the poor, and sacrificing your own physical life.

These acts may bring a measure of profit and help to someone else, but they won't do anything for us – they won't make us anything. These great acts don't make us someone great – it's love that makes us something and makes life great. And that love doesn't even originate with us, but it's God's love within us that brings value. We can't take credit for anything; all glory goes to Him.

At the end of it all, the only things that matter are love and what love produces. No matter what we may accomplish in life, without love, we are as nothing. It's love that gives our life value.

Love Definitions

The rest of chapter 13 defines divine love and love's responses; these are to define us. We are love children of a love God, and we possess a love nature; love is how we live. We choose to be dominated and governed by this great law of love, for love is the law of the new creature in Christ.

Love is the prescription that will make every home to be as Heaven on earth and every marriage a joy.

For those with problems in their marriage, my spiritual father would prescribe that before getting out of bed in the morning and before falling asleep at night, spouses should confess these things to one another. "I am patient, I am kind, etc....." When love is given its proper place, what a difference it makes.

Meditating on these passages and making them part of our everyday life will give us the best life.

1 CORINTHIANS 13:4-8 (AMPC)
4   Love endures long and is patient and kind; love never is envious nor boils over with jealousy, is not boastful or vainglorious, does not display itself haughtily.
5   It is not conceited (arrogant and inflated with pride); it is not rude (unmannerly) and does not act unbecomingly. Love (God's love in us) does not insist on its own rights or its own way, for it is not self-seeking; it is not touchy or fretful or resentful; it takes no account of the evil done to it [it pays no attention to a suffered wrong].
6   It does not rejoice at injustice and unrighteousness, but rejoices when right and truth prevail.
7   Love bears up under anything and everything that comes, is ever ready to believe the best of every person, its hopes are fadeless under all circumstances, and it endures everything [without weakening].
8   Love never fails [never fades out or becomes obsolete or comes to an end]....

(KJV)
4   Charity suffereth long, and is kind; charity envieth not; charity vaunteth not itself, is not puffed up,
5   Doth not behave itself unseemly, seeketh not her own, is not easily provoked, thinketh no evil;
6   Rejoiceth not in iniquity, but rejoiceth in the truth;

7 Beareth all things, believeth all things, hopeth all things, endureth all things.
8 Charity never faileth....

Love Translations

(In the following section, with each definition of love are listed other translations, then a few comments. I am also substituting the word "love" for charity.)

Love suffereth long – (misc. translations)

- *love is patient*
- *love is slow to lose patience*
- *love is never tired of waiting*
- *love never gives up*

Love is patient, slow to lose patience, and is never tired of waiting. With the patience that love gives, we can outlast any opposition and anything that comes. Remember, patience is a flow of love, but it's also a fruit of the spirit. The enemy doesn't possess any attributes of love or any fruits of the spirit, therefore, we can outlast him with this powerful force of patience.

Because love is patient, it is patient to the end; it doesn't quit along the way, for it never gives up. Love is a finisher; it's faithful to the finish.

Patience will turn us into finishers. What we start, we will finish. We won't lose interest along the way, become distracted, and fall short of the finish.

Hebrews 6:12 tells us that we, *"...through faith and patience inherit the promises."* Patience keeps faith from giving up.

Love never gives up. Since love is patient, it never gives up. It never gives up on the Word, and it never gives up on what belongs to it in Christ; it holds fast to the Word and remains steadfast to the end, no matter what opposes it.

Love never gives up on others either, for divine love sees them through the eyes of faith; love sees what they can be. God does that with us. He doesn't give up on us, for He knows who He made us to be.

Patience must be most prevalent in the home, for the home is full of imperfect people who are still growing, learning, and developing. Patience gives them room to grow without pushing them down or destroying the peace of the home.

Love is also patient toward the plan of God for our life. If we are not patient toward God's plan coming to pass, we can get out ahead of God or formulate our own plan. There's a big price to pay in getting out of God's will. When we are walking in love, we won't permit impatience to lead us out of His will, for love is patient toward God's plan coming to pass.

Many mistakenly think that they are patiently waiting for God to come through for them, but it's really the other way around. He is the One being patient with us. He is waiting for us to mature, develop, and believe so that He can bring some things into manifestation for us.

To be impatient is to step out of love, but being patient holds us in the love of God.

Love is kind –

- *love is courteous*
- *love is kind, gentle, benign, pervading and penetrating the whole nature, mellowing all which would have been harsh and austere*
- *love has no loud words in her mouth*
- *love cares for others more than for self*
- *love looks for a way of being constructive*

Love is kind. Since love is patient and kind, love is kind while it's being patient – it's kind while it waits. To be unkind is to step outside of love.

That kindness should be most apparent in our home and not just reserved for those we meet in public who we may never see again. Since we live with our family, they should get the best version of us.

Love is kind to the lovely and the unlovely. Love doesn't change based on who it's dealing with, for love is based on the One in us, it's not based on others. Therefore, kindness is to be our way of life, no matter who we are dealing with.

If we were walking down the street and a blind man bumped into us, we would respond to him in kindness, for we realize he can't see. We must remember that Satan has blinded the minds of those who don't believe – they don't see right. In our kindness, we must overlook their blindness.

Love is courteous. Courtesy is a flow of love. God is a perfect gentleman. He will never violate someone's will. He will never force or make someone do something, even if it's in their best interest. That's why God's power meets faith. When we release faith, that is God's invitation to move on our behalf. He won't move in our life uninvited.

Since love is courteous, that courtesy should be seen in our home with our family; it's not just to be reserved for our public life, but courtesy should also flourish in our home life.

If Jesus came to physically stay in our home, we would show Him the utmost courtesy. We would serve Him joyfully, attending to any need He may have. Even so, if spouses would do the same thing to one another, treating one another as they would Jesus, what a difference it would make in the home.

If you wouldn't think it, say it, or do it to Jesus, don't think it, say it, or do it to your spouse – or to anyone else.

Love cares for others more than for self. Since this is true, then I am to be committed to your success more than I am to my own. We are to help and encourage one another along in every way we can. Your success is my success.

Love makes us more aware of the other person than we are of ourself. Love doesn't consider self before it considers the other guy. Anytime I'm thinking of myself first, I'm not walking in love. Before saying or doing something, love always thinks, *How is this going to affect the other guy?* The more Christ-like we are, the more conscious we are of others than ourselves.

When we have a lifestyle of walking in love, we seldom think of ourselves.

Love won't use our own faith and resources just for ourself, but we will also use them to help someone else get theirs. That's what God did for us in sending Jesus; He gave His own Son to supply our need. Love is always seeking ways to bless someone else.

Love looks for a way of being constructive. It takes longer to build up than it does to tear down. What took years to build can be torn down in moments.

Love builds people – it takes on the long, consistent work of building people up – it never pushes them down. Love helps make the other guy look good. If we are to walk in divine health, we must pull people up, not push them down.

It is said of Jesus, *"A bruised reed shall he not break..."* (Matt. 12:20). Jesus' delight is not in discarding what is damaged, but in seeing that which was broken or injured made whole. He lifted man. Love lifted us, therefore, we lift others – we help lift them into all that God wants them to be.

Love envieth not –

- *love knows neither envy nor jealousy*
- *love doesn't want what belongs to others*
- *love is not possessive*

Because we are "in Christ," we have all been blessed with abundance. His blessings don't belong to one more than another. They are available to all of us, and it's faith that lays hold of them.

Love doesn't need to be envious or jealous of what others may have, for love is leaning and drawing on God, not others.

Love is not disturbed when God prospers others.

Ephesians 1:3 tells us, *"Blessed be the God and Father of our Lord Jesus Christ, who hath blessed us with all spiritual blessings in heavenly places in Christ."* My favorite translation reads that God has blessed us, *"...with everything that Heaven itself enjoys!"* (Norlie). Think of it! Nothing of Heaven has been withheld from us. It all belongs to us now to enjoy! And it's with our faith that we lay hold of it. Jealousy will never add anything to us, but exercising our faith will!

Love is not possessive. We don't need to be possessive of the things we have. We can freely share as the Spirit leads us to or as we choose to be generous. If we won't give it, we probably aren't safe in having it. Things we refuse to part with hold us captive.

Divine love is not possessive of things, but it's also not possessive of people. How many times marriages and relationships have been torn up due to possessiveness and jealousy. That is the flow of the carnal man, but not the spiritual man.

Love vaunteth not itself –

- *love is not forward and self-assertive*
- *love makes no parade*
- *love is not boastful*
- *love does not brag*
- *love doesn't sing its own praises*
- *love doesn't strut*
- *love is not anxious to impress*
- *love doesn't put itself up as being important*

Love doesn't put on display what it has and does to be seen of men. Love doesn't brag on itself, its spirituality, its works, or its own opinions. Love doesn't put itself up front; it doesn't promote itself.

Love doesn't announce its own good deeds. If we tell the good we did to impress others, that's all the reward we will get for it.

When we renew our minds to who we are in Christ, we overcome a bad self-image and rid ourselves of the need to try to impress others.

Love is not puffed up –

- *love doesn't have a swelled head*
- *love is not conceited*
- *love is not arrogant*
- *love doesn't look down upon others*
- *love gives itself no airs*
- *love has no pride*

- *love is not proud*
- *love doesn't cherish inflated ideas of its own importance*

Love doesn't seek to take center stage so it can be seen by others. Conceit puts self up front, but love doesn't.

Love doesn't think of himself or his works as being more important than the next guy's.

<u>Love doth not behave itself unseemly</u> –

- *love doesn't behave unbecomingly*
- *love never does the graceless thing*
- *love never lacks courtesy*
- *love doesn't act improperly*
- *love is not ill mannered*
- *love has good manners*
- *love doesn't force itself on others*
- *love isn't indecent*
- *love's ways are ever fair*
- *love isn't rude*
- *love is not injurious*
- *love does not dishonor others*

Love has good manners – naturally and spiritually. Love not only has impeccable manners, but has spiritual etiquette and ethics that will not harm a brother. Love is honorable at all times and holds an etiquette that is unoffensive.

Love is not crude in its speech or behavior. Love isn't indecent in thought, in speech, in behavior, or in dress.

Love treats all people honorably, not because they are honorable, but because we and the love in us are honorable. We are to be true to the honor within by treating all people honorably.

<u>Love seeketh not her own</u> –

- *love isn't always "me first"*
- *love does not seek to aggrandize herself*
- *love is never selfish*
- *love takes no thought for itself*
- *love doesn't seek its own advantage*
- *love doesn't seek its own way*
- *love does not look out for its own interests*
- *love never pursues its own selfish interest*
- *love does not insist upon having its own will*
- *love doesn't think about itself*
- *love does not insist on its own rights*
- *love does not pursue selfish advantage*

Anytime we demand our own way, we step out of love.

Love doesn't think more of its own opinions or its own thoughts, but will lay down its own thoughts and opinions to make peace, as long as it doesn't violate God or His Word.

If we put ourself first in any way and at any time (even in a conversation), we are outside of love. Love doesn't try to look big in the eyes of others.

Love doesn't seek its own advantage by putting someone else down for their own gain. Love doesn't step on other people, using them as ladders to reach the top.

Love takes no thought for itself, therefore it doesn't get puffed up by compliments.

Love is not easily provoked –

- *love is never irritated*
- *love never irritably loses its temper*
- *love doesn't fly off the handle*
- *love does not blaze out in passionate anger*
- *love does not get angry at little things*
- *love is never resentful*
- *love is not touchy, fretful, or resentful*
- *love is not quick to take offense*

Offenses will be offered, but love won't take them.

One of the dangers of offense is that most of the time people don't realize they are offended or won't acknowledge it, therefore, offense can become deeply rooted. When offense is not addressed, it destroys relationships and families, and it hinders spiritual progress.

To be become offended is to step out of love.

Love has no association with anger or with mood swings. It doesn't use any of these things to try to control or manipulate people or relationships.

Love is never irritated and doesn't lose its temper. Love holds us steady and makes us consistent; love is in utter control of self. When people see us, they should know what version of us they will get – the love version.

Love thinketh no evil –

- *love does not brood over wrongs*
- *love does not nurse hurt feelings*
- *love is never resentful*
- *love does not hold grudges and will hardly even notice when others do it* (them) *wrong*
- *love never nurses its wrath to keep it warm*
- *love is never glad when others go wrong*
- *love pays no attention to a suffered wrong*
- *love takes no account of the evil done to it*
- *love doesn't keep a record of complaints*
- *love does not search for imperfections and faults in others*
- *love does not keep track of other people's wrongs*
- *love does not take into account a wrong suffered*
- *love doesn't keep score of the sins of others*
- *love keeps no score of wrongs*
- *if you love someone, you will be loyal to him no matter what the cost, and you will always expect the best of him and always stand your ground in defending him*

In 1 Peter 4:8, we are instructed, *"Above all things have intense and unfailing love for one another, for love COVERS a multitude of sins [FORGIVES and DISREGARDS the offenses of others]"* (AMPC).

Flesh wants to tell it, but love wants to cover it with silence. Love never tells or broadcasts the sins of others. Every unlovely thing should die when we hear it; without anyone to repeat it, it dies.

Love overlooks faults, and when faults are overlooked, the good is all that's left to see.

Love can't keep score, for it can't add – it has no accounting skills. Love can't keep score of sins because it refuses to see them. Love can't count because it has no memory of the past. It forgives and forgets, so there's nothing left to count. Since God doesn't keep score of our sins, we shouldn't keep score of someone else's.

We are to be silent concerning the sins of others, but not our own; we are to repent of our own.

When someone under our authority persists in sin, we are anointed to help them, but we are not anointed to tell it to others.

Suffered wrongs want our attention, but love won't give attention to a suffered wrong. It doesn't hold onto it, rehearse it, or tell it to others, for love doesn't want others to know the wrong suffered.

If we are to protect our health and live in divine health, we must forgive and forget, refuse offense, and refuse to tell the sins of another.

Love is not only saying the right thing, but leaving unsaid the wrong thing at the tempting moment.

When we know and focus on the goodness of someone else's heart, it helps us to overlook any flaws.

My spiritual father would state, "When I see someone who has spoken against me, I just treat them like they bragged on me."

No matter what someone has done to me, if I fail to walk in love, that is the greater sin.

Love rejoiceth not in iniquity, but rejoiceth in the truth –

- *love doesn't revel when others grovel, but takes pleasure in the flowering of truth*
- *love is not happy with evil, but is happy with the truth*
- *love does not gloat over other people's sins, but takes its delight in the truth*
- *love does not rejoice about injustice, but rejoices whenever the truth wins out*
- *love is not happy with evil, but it is full of joy when the truth is spoken*
- *love finds no pleasure in injustice done to others, but joyfully sides with the truth*
- *love takes no pleasure in wrong doings*
- *love does not keep account of evil or gloat over the wickedness of other people; on the contrary, love shares the joy of those who live by the truth*

Love doesn't delight in saying, "I told you so!"

Love takes no part in anything wrong; love's only pleasure is love.

Love beareth all things –

- *love puts up with anything*
- *love bears up under anything and everything that comes*
- *love can stand any kind of treatment*

- *love has the power of undergoing all things*
- *love keeps its own counsel*
- *there is nothing love can't face*
- *love knows no limit to its endurance*
- *love never gives up*
- *love never stops being patient*
- *love always protects*
- *love knows how to be silent*

The strength of love is most visible under opposition. No opposition is big enough to defeat love.

Love knows how to be silent. Love always protects the other guy with silence. Proverbs 10:12 tells us, "...*Love covereth all sins.*" There's no sin love can't cover.

<u>Love believeth all things</u> –

- *love has faith in all things*
- *love always trusts*
- *love never loses faith*
- *love trusts God always*
- *love is full of trust*
- *love has no end to its trust* (in God)
- *love trusts in God in every situation and expects God to act in all circumstances*
- *love has unquenchable faith*
- *love exercises faith in everything*
- *love's first instinct is to believe in people*
- *love is ever ready to believe the best of every person*

The unspiritual man believes the worst, but love believes the best.

The faith born of love is unstoppable – nothing can quench it.

Love believes all of God's words and promises.

To not walk in faith is to not walk in love, for love exercises faith in everything. "...*Whatsoever is not of faith is sin*" (Rom. 14:23). Love never stops believing. Love has faith in all things – no matter what the circumstance, love holds to faith.

Love hopeth all things –

- *love hopes for all things*
- *love always hopes*
- *love never stops hoping*
- *love is full of hope*
- *love has no fading of its hopes*
- *love's hopes are fadeless under all circumstances*
- *love never regards anyone or anything as hopeless*
- *love always looks for the best*
- *love never looks back*

No circumstance can change love's position; it always hopes.

Love always looks for the best – no matter how long and deep it has to search.

Love never looks back. It never looks back in the past of others or of self. It forgets what's behind. Guilt, condemnation, and shame are in the backward direction. Hope, faith, and love move forward.

Love endureth all things –

- *love always endures*
- *love never gives up*
- *love keeps going to the end*
- *love always remains strong*
- *love always perseveres*
- *love endures through every circumstance*
- *love is full of patient endurance*
- *love keeps going to the end*
- *love knows no limit to its endurance*
- *love gives us power to endure everything*
- *love endures everything without weakening*
- *nothing can happen that can break love's spirit*
- *love endures without limit*

Love gets stronger as it goes – not weaker. There's no power to win like the power love gives. It can outlast anything because love is the greatest force.

Love doesn't know how to quit. To quit is to step out of love, for love is a finisher.

Love is full of patient endurance. Love endures with the demeanor of patience.

<u>Love never faileth</u> –

- *love never ends*
- *love never dies*
- *nothing can destroy love*
- *love is never lost*
- *love never comes to an end*
- *love never falls down on its task*
- *love falleth never down*
- *love is eternal*
- *love shall never pass away*
- *love never fails [never fades out or becomes obsolete or comes to an end]*

COMPILED LIST OF LOVE DEFINITIONS

(For convenience, all definitions and various translations listed in this chapter are compiled below into one list. I would recommend making copies of these pages to meditate on.)

Love suffereth long – (misc. translations)

- *love is patient*
- *love is slow to lose patience*
- *love is never tired of waiting*
- *love never gives up*

Love is kind –

- *love is courteous*
- *love is kind, gentle, benign, pervading and penetrating the whole nature, mellowing all which would have been harsh and austere*
- *love has no loud words in her mouth*
- *love cares for others more than for self*
- *love looks for a way of being constructive*

Love envieth not –

- *love knows neither envy nor jealousy*
- *love doesn't want what belongs to others*
- *love is not possessive*

Love vaunteth not itself –

- *love is not forward and self-assertive*
- *love makes no parade*
- *love is not boastful*

- *love does not brag*
- *love doesn't sing its own praises*
- *love doesn't strut*
- *love is not anxious to impress*
- *love doesn't put itself up as being important*

<u>Love is not puffed up</u> –

- *love doesn't have a swelled head*
- *love is not conceited*
- *love is not arrogant*
- *love doesn't look down upon others*
- *love gives itself no airs*
- *love has no pride*
- *love is not proud*
- *love doesn't cherish inflated ideas of its own importance*

<u>Love doth not behave itself unseemly</u> –

- *love doesn't behave unbecomingly*
- *love never does the graceless thing*
- *love never lacks courtesy*
- *love doesn't act improperly*
- *love is not ill mannered*
- *love has good manners*
- *love doesn't force itself on others*
- *love isn't indecent*
- *love's ways are ever fair*
- *love isn't rude*
- *love is not injurious*
- *love does not dishonor others*

Love seeketh not her own –

- *love isn't always "me first"*
- *love does not seek to aggrandize herself*
- *love is never selfish*
- *love takes no thought for itself*
- *love doesn't seek its own advantage*
- *love doesn't seek its own way*
- *love does not look out for its own interests*
- *love never pursues its own selfish interest*
- *love does not insist upon having its own will*
- *love doesn't think about itself*
- *love does not insist on its own rights*
- *love does not pursue selfish advantage*

Love is not easily provoked –

- *love is never irritated*
- *love never irritably loses its temper*
- *love doesn't fly off the handle*
- *love does not blaze out in passionate anger*
- *love does not get angry at little things*
- *love is never resentful*
- *love is not touchy, fretful, or resentful*
- *love is not quick to take offense*

Love thinketh no evil –

- *love does not brood over wrongs*
- *love does not nurse hurt feelings*
- *love is never resentful*

- *love does not hold grudges and will hardly even notice when others do it* (them) *wrong*
- *love never nurses its wrath to keep it warm*
- *love is never glad when others go wrong*
- *love pays no attention to a suffered wrong*
- *love takes no account of the evil done to it*
- *love doesn't keep a record of complaints*
- *love does not search for imperfections and faults in others*
- *love does not keep track of other people's wrongs*
- *love does not take into account a wrong suffered*
- *love doesn't keep score of the sins of others*
- *love keeps no score of wrongs*
- *if you love someone, you will be loyal to him no matter what the cost, and you will always expect the best of him and always stand your ground in defending him*

Love rejoiceth not in iniquity, but rejoiceth in the truth –

- *love doesn't revel when others grovel, but takes pleasure in the flowering of truth*
- *love is not happy with evil, but is happy with the truth*
- *love does not gloat over other people's sins, but takes its delight in the truth*
- *love does not rejoice about injustice, but rejoices whenever the truth wins out*
- *love is not happy with evil, but it is full of joy when the truth is spoken*
- *love finds no pleasure in injustice done to others, but joyfully sides with the truth*

- *love takes no pleasure in wrong doings*
- *love does not keep account of evil or gloat over the wickedness of other people; on the contrary, love shares the joy of those who live by the truth*

Love beareth all things –

- *love puts up with anything*
- *love bears up under anything and everything that comes*
- *love can stand any kind of treatment*
- *love has the power of undergoing all things*
- *love keeps its own counsel*
- *there is nothing love can't face*
- *love knows no limit to its endurance*
- *love never gives up*
- *love never stops being patient*
- *love always protects*
- *love knows how to be silent*

Love believeth all things –

- *love has faith in all things*
- *love always trusts*
- *love never loses faith*
- *love trusts God always*
- *love is full of trust*
- *love has no end to its trust* (in God)
- *love trusts in God in every situation and expects God to act in all circumstances*
- *love has unquenchable faith*
- *love exercises faith in everything*

- *love's first instinct is to believe in people*
- *love is ever ready to believe the best of every person*

Love hopeth all things –

- *love hopes for all things*
- *love always hopes*
- *love never stops hoping*
- *love is full of hope*
- *love has no fading of its hopes*
- *love's hopes are fadeless under all circumstances*
- *love never regards anyone or anything as hopeless*
- *love always looks for the best*
- *love never looks back*

Love endureth all things –

- *love always endures*
- *love never gives up*
- *love keeps going to the end*
- *love always remains strong*
- *love always perseveres*
- *love endures through every circumstance*
- *love is full of patient endurance*
- *love keeps going to the end*
- *love knows no limit to its endurance*
- *love gives us power to endure everything*
- *love endures everything without weakening*
- *nothing can happen that can break love's spirit*
- *love endures without limit*

<u>Love never faileth</u> –

- *love never ends*
- *love never dies*
- *nothing can destroy love*
- *love is never lost*
- *love never comes to an end*
- *love never falls down on its task*
- *love falleth never down*
- *love is eternal*
- *love shall never pass away*
- *love never fails [never fades out or becomes obsolete or comes to an end]*

Prayer of Salvation

Heavenly Father, I come to You in the Name of Jesus. Your Word says, *"...him that cometh to me I will in no wise cast out"* (John 6:37). So I know You won't cast me out, but You will take me in, and I thank You for it.

You said in Your Word, *"...If thou shalt confess with thy mouth the Lord Jesus, and shalt believe in thine heart that God hath raised him from the dead, thou shalt be saved. For whosoever shall call upon the name of the Lord shall be saved"* (Rom. 10:9 & 13).

I believe in my heart that Jesus Christ is the Son of God. I believe Jesus died for my sins and was raised from the dead so I can be in right-standing with God. I am calling upon His Name, the Name of Jesus, so I know, Father, that You save me now.

Your Word says, *"...with the heart man believeth unto righteousness; and with the mouth confession is made unto salvation"* (Rom. 10:10). I do believe with my heart, and I confess Jesus now as my Lord. Therefore, I am saved! Thank You, Father.

Please write us and let us know that you have just been born again. When you write, ask to receive our salvation booklets.

To contact us, please email us at
dm@dufresneministries.org
or write to:
Dufresne Ministries
P.O. Box 1010
Murrieta, CA 92564

How To Be Filled With the Holy Spirit

Acts 2:38 reads, *"...Repent, and be baptized every one of you in the name of Jesus Christ for the remission of sins, and ye shall receive the GIFT of the Holy Ghost."* The Holy Ghost is a gift that belongs to each one of God's people. Jesus is the gift God gave the whole world, but the Holy Spirit is a gift that belongs only to God's people.

Jesus told His disciples, *"But ye shall receive POWER, after that the Holy Ghost is come upon you: and ye shall be witnesses unto me..."* (Acts 1:8). When you're baptized with the Holy Spirit, you receive supernatural power that enables you to live victoriously.

Indwelling vs. Infilling

When you're born again, you receive the indwelling of the Person of the Holy Spirit. Romans 8:16 tells us, *"The Spirit itself* (Himself) *beareth witness with our spirit, that we are the children of God."* When you're born again, you know it because the Spirit bears witness with your spirit that you are a child of God; He confirms it to you. He's able to bear witness with your spirit because He's in you; you are *indwelt* by the Spirit of God.

But the Word of God speaks of another experience subsequent to the new birth that belongs to every believer, and that is to be baptized with the Holy Spirit, or to receive the *infilling* of the Holy Spirit.

God wants you to be full and overflowing with the Spirit. Being filled with the Spirit is likened to being full of water. Just because you had one drink of water doesn't mean you're full of water. At the new birth, you received the indwelling of the Spirit – a drink of water. But now God wants you to be filled to overflowing – be filled with His Spirit, baptized with the Holy Ghost.

> **ACTS 2:1-4**
> **1 And when the day of Pentecost was fully come, they were all with one accord in one place.**
> **2 And suddenly there came a sound from heaven as of a rushing mighty wind, and it filled all the house where they were sitting.**
> **3 And there appeared unto them cloven tongues like as of fire, and it sat upon each of them.**
> **4 And they were all FILLED with the Holy Ghost, and BEGAN TO SPEAK WITH OTHER TONGUES, as the Spirit gave them utterance.**

When these disciples were filled with the Holy Ghost, they began to speak with other tongues as the Spirit gave them utterance; they spoke in a language unknown to them. Today, when a believer is filled with the Holy Ghost, they will speak with other tongues too. These are not words that come from the mind of man, but they are words given by the Holy

Spirit; these words float up from their spirit within, and the person then speaks those out.

What is the benefit of being filled with the Holy Ghost with the evidence of speaking in other tongues? First Corinthians 14:2 reads, *"For he that speaketh in an unknown tongue speaketh not unto men, but unto God...."* When you're speaking in other tongues, you're speaking to God – it is a divine means of communicating with your Heavenly Father. This is one of many great benefits.

> **MATTHEW 7:7-11**
> **7   Ask, and it shall be given you...**
> **8   FOR EVERY ONE THAT ASKETH RE-CEIVETH...**
> **9   ...what man is there of you, whom if his son ask bread, will he give him a stone?**
> **10 Or if he ask a fish, will he give him a serpent?**
> **11 If ye then, being evil, know how to give good gifts unto your children, HOW MUCH MORE SHALL YOUR FATHER WHICH IS IN HEAVEN GIVE GOOD THINGS TO THEM THAT ASK HIM?**

In this passage, Jesus is saying that when you ask God for something, you shall receive it! Believe that He will give you that which you ask for. When you ask God for something good, He won't give you something that will harm you; He will give you the good thing you ask for. The baptism of the Holy Spirit is a good gift, and when you ask God to fill you with the Holy Spirit, you won't receive a wrong spirit; you will receive this good gift, the gift of the Holy Spirit.

Once you receive the gift of the Holy Ghost, you can yield to this gift any time, speaking in other tongues as often as you choose; you don't have to wait for God to move on you. The more you speak in other tongues, the more you will benefit from this gift. By continuing to speak in other tongues on a daily basis, you will be able to maintain a Spirit-filled life; you will live full of the Spirit.

The more you take time to speak in other tongues, the deeper you'll move into the things of God.

(For more teaching on being filled with the Holy Spirit, I recommend the mini-book, *Why Tongues?* by Kenneth E. Hagin.)

Prayer To Receive the Holy Spirit

"Father, I see that the gift of the Holy Spirit belongs to Your children. So, I come to You to receive this gift. I received my salvation by faith, so I receive the gift of the Holy Spirit by faith. I believe I receive the Holy Spirit now! Since I'm filled with the Holy Spirit now, I expect to speak in other tongues as the Spirit gives me utterance, just like those in Acts 2 on the Day of Pentecost. Thank You for filling me with the Holy Ghost."

Now, words that the Spirit of God gives you will float up from your spirit. You are the one who must open your mouth and speak those words out. The words will not come to your mind, but they will float up from your spirit. Speak those out freely.